INCOME AND WEALTH

David Parker Essays

Volume One

Printed in the United States of America

First Printing, 2021

ISBN-13: 978-1-951805-90-6 print edition
ISBN-13: 978-1-951805-91-3 ebook edition

Waterside Productions
2055 Oxford Ave
Cardiff, CA 92007
www.waterside.com

DEDICATION

To my wife, Christiane, who reminds me every day that
everything I'm looking for is right in front of me.

CONTENTS

FOREWORD

That income and wealth are two completely separate matters is an idea I have been thinking about for 40 years. About 30 years ago I started to write about it. My wife took one look and said, "I think you'd better take a class in economics."

So, I went to Golden Gate University and took 67 units of math and economics. I then wrote seven 100-page essays: "Insider Trading," "Social Security (both of which were published in the *Journal of Law and Business*), "The Environment," "Healthcare," "The 2008 Financial Crisis," "The Euro" and "Economic Commentary on the Budget of the San Francisco Unified School District" (accepted as a master's thesis for an MS degree in economics). I also wrote a "Letter to the Editor" in *The Economist* about the 2008 Financial Crisis, published alongside a letter by the economic advisor to the Prime Minister of England.

Now, I have completed "Income and Wealth," my original theme. The book includes business and economic insights carried with me since the age of 12, in addition to 40 years' experience teaching inner-city public schools, 40 years a professional musician and 40 years of real estate investment.

My hope is that "Income and Wealth" opens up a world of understanding. In this sense, please don't skip the endnotes. In themselves, they are a second book.

David Parker
San Francisco
December 2020

1

INTRODUCTION

Income and Wealth

For an individual, the most fundamental of all economic goals is financial independence—freedom from worrying about the state of the economy, from following the news every day, from producing a product or making a profit. Financial independence is possible for anyone because there is no relation between earning a living and acquiring assets, no relation between income and wealth. An employee at McDonald's making minimum wage can become financially independent within ten years.

Consider Andrew Carnegie: A young immigrant from Scotland, in 1848, without money or contacts, within a few years of arrival in America had acquired most of the nation's steel mills. Alone in his room, he read voraciously about the laws of money and economics. Pacing his library, sending a few telegrams, he applied what he learned. Soon afterward and for the rest of his life, Carnegie, the richest man in America, arguably in the world, even today, spent his time giving that money away, building and endowing the nation's public libraries, for one.

Consider my grandfather: An immigrant from Austria, in 1938, who had to leave everything behind, paced the house. Until my grandmother couldn't stand it any longer and told him to go out and do something. He came back with four movie theaters.[1]

For Carnegie as for my grandfather there was no relation between the wealth they acquired and the income they had. Their wealth did not come from savings but from investment, the purchase of assets with leverage, when possible, borrowing up to 100 percent of value.[2] (Most people purchase with their savings as a down payment and borrow the balance, but professional investors will borrow the entire amount—the leveraged buyout.)

It is not a coincidence that Andrew Carnegie and my grandfather made their money in America; the opportunity is here, the result of the certainty of this country's social, political and economic freedom, precisely what attracts creative, ambitious and entrepreneurial people.[3]

John D. Unruh, Jr., in *The Plains Across, The Overland Emigrants and the Trans-Mississippi West, 1840-60*, states that "the importance of privation, bravery, creativity, determination to solve problems of danger… [are those] characteristics that drained Europe of much of its vitality and made the U.S. an empire extending from coast to coast." To Unruh, those characteristics have not yet been bred out of American culture.[4]

Carnegie and my grandfather applied the laws of money and economics to acquire assets. But they also had business experience. In *The Empire of Business*, a series of lectures in 1902 at Columbia University, Carnegie states emphatically that preparation for business means to start at the bottom and learn everything.[5] To Carnegie, those wishing to make a fortune are wasting their time going to college. Professional sports are the analogy today. Certain careers start when one is young, when the

2

body and mind are agile. In exchange, success comes quickly, leaving a lifetime afterward for study.[6]

My first experience with the idea that there may be no relation between income and wealth came as a child. I read in the newspaper about the death of an old waiter at the St. Francis Hotel in San Francisco, that it was discovered he had amassed a fortune and I remember thinking, "How was that possible? Waiters don't earn a lot of money."

My second experience came at my first public school teaching assignment. I regularly dropped by to talk with the school custodian at his tiny office, listen to Pavarotti, debate his claim of the superiority of Italian over French cuisine and to sense his joy at coming to work at dawn so he could turn on the heat and talk with early arriving students and teachers. It never occurred to me until he revealed it that he was not working for the money, that he owned four apartment buildings from which he derived ample cash flow.

McDonald's

So, like the custodian, and probably the waiter, why can't a young couple working at McDonald's at minimum wage become financially independent in seven years? Because at minimum wage, it takes ten years.[7] It works like this:

If an employee at McDonald's earns $10.00 an hour,[8] ten hours a day, six days a week, that's $600 per week. If the spouse also works at McDonald's, the $600 becomes $1,200, times four, $4,800 a month, $57,600 a year. For ten years, the two employees save half of what they earn: $28,800 a year.

At the end of each year that $28,800 savings is invested as a down payment on a $150,000 asset, say, a one-third interest in a $450,000 residence. At the end of ten years, ten such $150,000 assets, each appreciating at 4% per year, will be worth $1,872,856,

3

and will generate $93,746 annual cash flow, a 39% annual rate of return on total cash invested of $288,000 ($28,800 times 10). The spreadsheet below shows equity build up for Asset No. 1:

Asset No. 1

Year No.	Cash	Loan amount	Original investment	4% Appreciation (compounded)	Asset value end of year	Annual loan amortization (4% int/30-yr)	1% Cash flow
1	$28,800	$121,200	$150,000	$6,000	$156,000	$2,134	$1,500
2		119,066		6,240	162,240	2,221	1,560
3		116,845		6,489	168,729	2,311	1,622
4		114,534		6,739	175,468	2,406	1,687
5		112,138		7,018	182,486	2,504	1,754
6		109,634		7,299	189,785	2,606	1,824
7		107,028		7,591	197,376	2,712	1,897
8		104,316		7,895	205,271	2,822	1,973
9		101,494		8,210	213,481	2,937	2,052
10		98,557		8,539	222,020	3,057	2,134
							18,003

The owners' equity in Asset No. 1 is the value of the asset at the end of year ten: $222,020, less the ending loan balance of $98,557, plus the total cash flow $18,003:

$$\$222,020$$
$$- \ 98,557$$
$$+ \ \underline{18,003}$$
$$\$141,463$$

At the end of ten years, the equity in Asset No. 2, purchased one year later, is the value of Asset No. 1 built up through year nine. The equity in Asset No. 3 is the value of Asset No. 1 up through year eight. Asset No. 4 through year seven, continuing to Asset No. 10 through year one:

Total value of the assets:

Asset No. 1	$222,020
" 2	213,481
" 3	205,271
" 4	197,376
" 5	189,785
" 6	182,486
" 7	175,468
" 8	168,486
" 9	162,240
" 10	156,000
	$1,872,856

Total value of the loans:	Total value of the cash flows:
$ 98,557	$18,003
101,494	15,869
104,316	13,817
107,028	11,920
109,634	10,023
112,138	8,199
114,534	6,495
116,845	4,758
119,066	3,136
121,200	1,576
$699,043	$93,746

At the end of ten years, the owners' equity is the total value of Assets 1 through 10, $1,872,856, less the total value of the loans, $699,043, plus the total value of all the cash flows, $93,746.

$$\begin{array}{r} \$1,872,856 \\ -\ \ 699,812 \\ +\ \ \ \ 93,746 \\ \hline \$1,267,559 \end{array}$$

If our McDonald's couple then sells their ten assets and purchases a single $1,267,559 asset that earns 4% interest per annum, their yearly income will be $50,702. (Or, if they keep the ten assets, the return is the same.)

The young couple no longer need maintain their Spartan lifestyle (living on $28,800 a year). Now they can live on their annual cash flow of $50,702 a year. They are financially independent.

Of course, $50,702 a year is minimal financial independence. Yearly income could be greater under other circumstances: if the couple each earned twice minimum wage, $20.00 an hour; or worked twice as long, 20 years (because they couldn't keep up the Spartan lifestyle); or were active in the management and development of their real estate so that the value of the real estate increased at more than four percent a year. The point: even at minimum wage, it's possible to acquire enough assets so that wealth is no longer a function of income, rather, that income is a function of wealth.

For a more accurate (and surprising) accounting of the above example, see Appendix B.

Poverty

Besides there being no relation between income and wealth, there is no relation between income and poverty. People think there is, and have always thought so, which is why the Middle Ages lasted 1,000 years; why the Catholic Church accepted poverty as destiny (preaching, "The meek shall inherit the earth"); why the Middle Ages are known as the Dark Ages. Around 1600, finally, Francis Bacon declared that it was possible to progress out of serfdom, that people could easily improve their lives by using the technology of the day, by asking questions and, just as important, by requiring proof of the answers. Bacon is credited for the "scientific method" and for the idea of "progress."

Poverty is a state of mind. According to surveys by the United Nations Children's Emergency Fund (UNICEF) and U.S. Agency for International Development (USAID), there are many elements to poverty: education—no one in a family having completed five years of schooling, or some children never having attended primary school; health—child mortality and families who are malnourished; living standard—no electricity, no decent toilet or latrine, no easy access to drinking water, dirt, sand or dung floors, cooking with dung, wood or charcoal, no car or truck and only one of the following: a radio, television, telephone, bike, motorbike or refrigerator. By this standard, no American lives in poverty.[9]

2

SOME ECONOMIC PRINCIPLES

Timeless Rates of Return

Again, a principal theme of this book is that there is no relation between income and wealth, between earning a living and acquiring assets. The idea derives from the natural laws of money and economics.1

One such law is the Efficient Market Hypothesis: *in a competitive economy, all investments produce the same rate of return.* What this means is that it's not important what investment you make; it's important only that you make an investment.

Throw a dart at the stock market page; buy whatever company it lands on. That company will produce the same rate of return as any other. Why? Because in an efficient market, whenever a stock produces an above-market return, buyers rush to purchase it; within seconds, its price rises such that its return is again equal to the others. Observe traffic backed up on a freeway; when one lane starts to flow, cars move over to that lane, and, right away all lanes are moving again at the same pace. No need to invest in a different lane; profit is zero.

Hidden, then, in the Efficient Market Hypothesis is the fact that not only do all investments produce the same rate of return, but that in the long run, all profit is zero. Why? Because basic rates of return are not profit. They are the time value of money—historically one to two percent for savings, two to three percent for mortgage lending, three to five percent for venture capital. When a rate is higher, risk is higher.[2]

But what about high income, even unconscionably high income? That also has nothing to do with a rate of return: *high income is entrepreneurial compensation*, that portion of a firm's total revenue generated by a particular individual. In professional sports, athletes, no differently than CEOs are paid a portion of the revenue they personally generate—perhaps two percent of that revenue.[3] The high compensation, however, does not last. It comes at the early stages of a product and drops off as the creative entrepreneur starts to generate less income. At that time the entrepreneur may leave, and the replacement CEO has but one function: *to slow down the rate at which the firm is losing market share*.

So, why are some CEOs paid $100 million a year? The only answer is supply and demand. Market reality is that few people are capable of holding a large corporation together. [See Appendix D, "Entrepreneurial Mindset."] The natural law of demand, that *price is a function of demand*, forces their compensation to be bid up. It may take a $100 million a year to entice a multi-millionaire to give up those mornings at the country estate reading *Essays* of Montaigne, setting up childrens' birthday parties in the afternoon, or what comedian Jerry Seinfeld calls "Gone Out, Left Family" (GOLF).

The correct insight is that wealth does not come from salary: *wealth is a function of acquiring assets through the use of leverage* —purchasing an asset with a down payment, borrowing the balance —*the* reason someone on a modest salary can (at that salary level) be as financially independent as someone on a high salary.[4]

Another important principle is that not only are rates of return timeless, but that rates of return are not profit. Every cost increase to business, therefore, adds to those rates. Taxation and regulation, the cost of solving social and economic problems through the political process, *has* to be passed back to the consumer. Unfortunately, that inefficiency leads to anti-competitive business behavior, for example, to large corporations with their low long-run-average-costs absorbing the added costs and then buying up the smaller firms that cannot. Thus, the consequence of legislation such as Sarbanes-Oxley and Dodd-Frank is that they push businesses to become too-big-to-fail, to become monopolies, and the nation to become a corporate state. The corporate state, socialism from the right, is a handful of corporations picked to carry out government policy (like in the 1930s and '40s in Italy, Germany and Japan). Watch out, then, when large corporations pretend not to want regulation. Like Uncle Remus' Brer Rabbit, they will yell, "Oh, whatever you do, please, please, don't regulate us!" [5]

Government intervention in the economy has to be accounted for: it disturbs real rates of return—the time value of money at risk—and disturbs the market's self-correction process— its natural ability to adjust to price change. Producers see rising price signals as a genuine increase in demand for goods and services, and so, increase production.[6] Once they realize the price increase was an adjustment to taxation and regulation, that it was artificial—inflation, artificial demand—and that they are holding unsold inventory, they will halt production. Hello, recession.

With recession, however, other problems arise: unemployment, and Keynesian pressure on government to do something about it, to stimulate demand through deficit spending. Years later, when everyone realizes that those interventions had no effect, to the contrary, that it was taxation and regulation that caused the recession, that along with belt-tightening, the solution should have been to reduce taxation and regulation, *then* the recession will turn around.[7] The following timeline of the U.S. economy glaringly reveals that government intervention in the 1930s greatly prolonged the Great Depression. The huge black mass that marks the 1930s' Great Depression, the only huge black mass, also marks the only economic downturn in which government intervened. The 1930s recession, about to end in 1933 (before any of the New Deal programs kicked in—see the large gap in that black mass after 1935), because of government policy that restricted the money supply and curtailed international trade, turned into the Great Depression. The Depression continued until 1942, and would have continued another ten years had it not been for World War II.

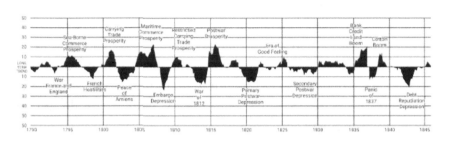

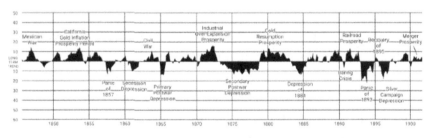

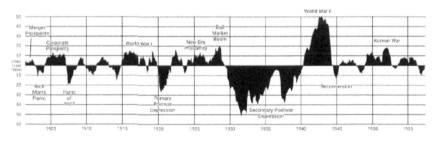

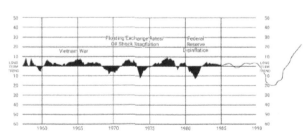

Was it the massive spending for World War II that ended the Depression? Yes, but only because the timing was right: it came at the end. At the onset of a depression, massive government spending is useless: depressions and recessions are free-market phenomena that must run their course.[8] Recessions are the result of an overexpansion of credit, a natural human phenomenon that, like a wound to the body, cannot heal faster than nature allows. Only at the end of a healing period might massive injection of vitamins have an effect.[9] See "Keynesian Economics" below.

However, before a discussion of Keynesian economics— economics based on the belief that a modern economy must have a governmental component, that social workers and politicians should be given a say—one must understand that to Keynesians it doesn't matter that an advanced industrialized economy is too complex to be managed (in that no one can possibly manage 300 million people making decisions encompassing billions of interacting bits of information per second), or that individuals in a free society prefer to make those decisions for themselves. Keynesians are more interested in principles of social justice and wealth redistribution, and in the "benefits" of deficit spending. They are not interested in the adverse consequences (think European socialism). They are not interested in the economic principles that make it possible for a McDonald's employee to become financially independent. Why? Because Keynesian economics is not economics; it's social policy; it's wealth redistribution.[10] Wealth as a function of acquiring assets, *that's* economics. Financial independence from acquiring assets through leverage, *that's* economics. McDonald's, *that's* economics.

13

Keynesian Economics

Not only rates of return, but so, too, principles of capital formation are timeless. Only an economist could come up with the idea, "paradox of thrift," that too much saving stops consumption and thus prolongs a recession. So counter to good business sense, it shows why economists should stick to analyses which require no knowledge of business—for example, to intellectual issues concerning trade, or to the study of how individuals transform natural resources into final products. Economists should stick to the microeconomic subject of who it is exactly that creates an economy: suppliers—that an economy is a supply-side phenomenon, that supply is a function of money invested, at risk, and that an economy functions only when suppliers are willing to act. No matter how much money demanders have, no matter how much money government provides (to stimulate supply or demand), if suppliers are not confident, they will not produce. They will not act until they believe that demand by government or consumers is real, and won't be retracted.[11]

> What a country wants to make it richer is never consumption, but production. Where there is the latter, we may be sure that there is no want of the former.

The quote is by John Stewart Mill, 1830. In 1803, J. B. Say had said the same, Say's Law, that "supply creates its own demand." Then, in 1936, John Maynard Keynes said the very opposite: to reverse a recession, nations must consume as much as possible, spend more than they earn, and keep borrowing—until the recession is over.[12] Not true. To reverse a recession, bad financial instruments and surplus inventory from the economy's over expansion must first be sold off. Then, as population grows, as old inventory wears out, as needs return for genuine financial instruments, i.e., farmers who hedge the price of their own crops, new demand emerges naturally. For production to resume, demand must be real.[13]

People on the Left, Keynesians, believe that to reverse a recession, government, by borrowing, must put people to work. Why? Because when the newly employed start spending income on goods and services, the recession will end; out of real employment will arise real demand. Whoa! Neither the employment nor the demand is real; neither stem spontaneously from the market; this can't last. Furthermore, government does this without any evidence that the newly employed will spend their new money rather than hoard it, without any evidence that if they spent it there would be a multiplier effect, that $1.00 in increased spending would lead to $1.25 in additional demand, thus additional employment. Eighty years after *The General Theory of Employment, Interest and Money*, there still is no evidence that during a recession, fiscal policy, increased government spending, and the lowering of tax rates, has an effect. Despite the fact that most economists advocate monetary policy—increasing the money supply—Keynesians still advocate fiscal policy.[14]

Worse, when the economy is not in recession, Keynesians believe that citizens should still be required to give up some amount of personal consumption for the benefit of society-as-a-whole (through taxation, how socialist economics are created), and, of course, that wealth should be distributed more fairly (see redistributed), to the point of not only employing all resources, but employing them so efficiently that it is not possible to produce more of one thing without producing less of something else. The production possibility curve demonstrates this well-known principle of opportunity costs:

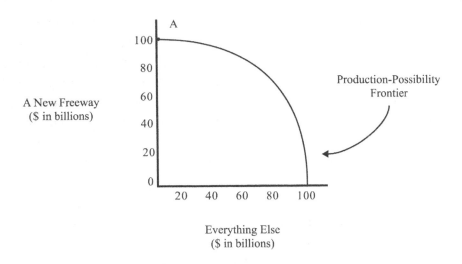

The above production-possibility frontier of $100 billion shows that building a $100 billion freeway means that nothing else can be built (Point A on the above curve). Not true; resources are not limited. At a particular moment in time they are in short supply, but then rationing them is the purpose of a market economy: fluctuating prices provide information about the availability of trade resources such that, as prices rise, only the most efficient firms purchase them—the only fair way for resources to be distributed.

What the Left doesn't understand is that the quickest least painful way to end a recession is to let it run its course. Let the market correct itself! During the process tax revenue will be lower, therefore, so, too, government expenditures. If politicians can't decide what to cut, they should just cut everything at the same rate. Taking too much time to determine which programs not to cut is cruel: it prolongs the recession.[15]

Trade

Economics is about trade—about voluntarily giving up one thing for something else that one values more. Whether between individuals or nations, trade is for *gain*.[16]

According to Adam Smith, *The Wealth of Nations*, 1776, trade is what human beings do—"truck, barter and trade"—carry things around (including ideas) with the hope of improving the situation. What is carried around is surplus production, *the definition of capital*—the free trade of which is called capitalism. Reality is that

> The history of humankind has been the struggle for survival. Until quite recently, humanity spent virtually its entire life at labor, providing the food, clothing and shelter required for life. Standards of living seldom rose very far above a subsistence level. Humankind was subject to famine, disease, natural calamities, and social unrest, all resulting in widespread human suffering.
>
> Such conditions were found in the early colonial settlements in America, but these communities soon developed an economic structure beyond the subsistence level, thus creating a higher standard of living. In the 19th century, America underwent further economic growth which in turn brought about prosperity unprecedented in previous history.
>
> Such economic miracles have affected but an infinitesimal fraction of the human race. Indeed, the majority of those fortunate enough to experience life significantly above a bare subsistence level are actually living at the present time, and then in just a few developed countries, notably the United States. It is *economic growth* [italics added] which has been the basis for most of our achievements above and beyond the biological struggle for existence. Until society generated

resources [capital] exceeding those required for mere survival, little opportunity could occur for learning, science, art—indeed, all of those aspects of life that we identify with civilization.[17]

But let government limit trade—decrease economic growth —and the standard of living drops, immediately. It is a mistake to believe that once a nation is rich, it can switch its focus toward equality of income and wealth—away from protecting the free economy which made the wealth possible, to a socialist economy where economic considerations are balanced with social considerations. This transition from capitalism to communism is what Karl Marx had in mind.[18] (See Appendix C, "Capitalism.")

From the perspective of raising the standard of living, a nation should not focus on social considerations, on, for example, inequality of income and wealth. Inequality of income and wealth is *the* actual engine of a dynamic economy (the driver of which is the creative entrepreneur). Greed plays a part, but is irrelevant— communists are greedier than capitalists. What's relevant is the reality of *unlimited economic expansion.* Economic growth needs increased capital (generated in a market economy), but the essence of economic growth, the very reason it is unlimited, is that it is based on increased knowledge: new ideas in production, product and technology.[19]

––––––––––

The study of trade is the subject of economics. The first clear articulation of economics as a subject is *The Wealth of Nations* (1776), in which Adam Smith explains that the market, not government, coordinates the economic activities of individuals so as to maximize the welfare of society as a whole. With trade always possible, the market, then, is the natural law basis of individual freedom.

18

One of Smith's major insights is that in a market system, no external coercion is required to achieve cooperation among private individuals.

> Each individual who intends only his own gain is led by an invisible hand to promote an end which was no part of his intention. Nor is it always the worse for society that it was no part of it. By pursuing his own interest he frequently promotes that of the society more effectively than when he really intends to promote it. I have never known much good done by those who affected to trade for the public good.[20]

Smith grasped the notion that economic freedom is the prerequisite to political freedom. He grasped that voluntary cooperation between individuals leaves very little room for political power, very little for government to do. Real power, then, economic power, is dispersed among every member of society. When it is concentrated in the hands of government, the result is tyranny. *That* is what Thomas Jefferson and the Founding Fathers worried about, why they dispersed power into three branches of government—to prevent either a majority or a minority from using government to advance its own interests. To the Founders, the purpose of the Constitution was to provide a clear set of rules for preventing government from replacing citizens in the creation of the nation's welfare.[21]

The American colonies, populated by a self-reliant people who naturally took individual initiative, benefited from economic freedom. It was Alexis de Tocqueville who first used the term *individualism* to describe American society, what he believed held the society together, love of prosperity and the spirit of commercial enterprise.[22]

Again, the Founding Fathers understood that the pursuit of self-interest would go too far when it led to the creation of powerful special-interest groups. James Madison anticipated this perfectly:

Those who hold and those who are without property have ever formed distinct interest in society...a landed interest, a manufacturing interest, a mercantile interest, and a money interest, with many lesser interests, grow up of necessity in civilized nations, and divide themselves into different classes, activated by different sentiments and views. The regulation of these various and interfering interests involves the spirit of party and factor in the necessary and ordinary operations of government.

...the public good is disregarded in the conflicts of rival parties, and ... measures are often decided, not according to the rules of justice and the rights of the minority party, but by the superior force of an interested and overbearing majority. However anxiously we may wish that these complaints had no foundation; the evidence of known facts will not permit us to deny that they are in some degree true.[23]

James Madison understood that interest groups would use the power of government to maximize their own ends at the expense of the interests of society as a whole, *and*, that that would lead to an expansion of government. One of the world's great political documents, *The Federalist Papers No. 10*, by Madison, states that division of power exists precisely to protect minority interests. Today, enormous expansion of government, centralization of power, and regulation of commerce (nineteenth century progressivism stamped into place in the 1930s and 1960s), have put the U.S. at risk of losing not only its great wealth, but its underlying reliance on individualism.

———

Nations are also at risk of losing their wealth when they make the mistake of trying to produce everything themselves and then try to protect domestic employment by closing their economy to world trade. Rather, nations should trade according to comparative advantage—produce those things that cost them less to produce than the nations they trade with. David Ricardo, in *On the Principles of Political Economy and Taxation* (1817), is credited for that insight.

Britain, for example, should not produce port wine; at a minimum, it has the wrong climate. And Portugal should not produce automobiles; it does not have the factories or trained labor to match Britain. For Portugal to produce port wine rather than automobiles and be competitive, wages might drop from $15 to $10 an hour, but, for Britain, wages *would* drop from $25 to $15 an hour. Portugal has the comparative advantage: it may or may not cost Portugal $5 an hour, but it would definitely cost Britain $10 an hour. Even if Britain produced better wine, Portugal still has the comparative advantage: comparative advantage is relative, not absolute. *That* is the brilliance of the theory.[24]

The U.S., with its highly paid and creative workforce, should produce products that require advanced technology. Why? Because it costs the U.S. more to produce low skilled goods, textiles, for example, than it does most other counties, Mexico, for example. It costs Mexico nothing to switch from agriculture to textiles. It costs the U.S. $100 an hour to switch from Silicon Valley research to textile production.[25]

Germany should produce highly engineered industrial products. Germany has a cultural affinity for efficiency, and for the trades—from the age of fourteen, German workers apprentice in manufacturing. Germany is unrivaled in the production of high-quality industrial goods at a low price.[26]

Japan, too, should produce high technology and highly engineered products. It should not produce agricultural products. It should not produce rice. With inefficient farming on hillside plots, Japan cannot compete with California, where abundant flat floodable land produces rice on an industrial scale at half the price.[27]

Adam Smith, David Ricardo, J. B. Say, Carl Menger, Alfred Marshall, these economists gave the world the language and principles of economics. Yet, to what extent have these principles always been known? In sixth century Babylon, when money evolved, so too did secondary markets—markets for secured collateral, including real estate, where matters of title (on stone tablets) were of public record. And comparative advantage has early roots. Athens in the 6th century, a rising power whose economy was in disarray but with wise leadership, gave Solon, a philosopher and successful merchant, total control. Solon told Athenians to produce nothing but olive oil and high-cost pottery. With land in Attica good only for olive trees, and with the best artists all living in Athens—and with their prowess in shipping— Solon told them to produce for the world market.[28]

Had Solon not forced this economic change, 5th century Athens might not have flourished to the extent it did. Today the world flourishes because all economists agree that nations should trade according to comparative advantage and that barriers to trade lower economic growth. It is the main reason to study political economy: so that citizens have the correct arguments to persuade governments not to intervene in the economy.

Consider the 1908 platform of the Republican Party:

> The true principle of protection is best maintained by the imposition of such duties as would equalize the difference between the cost of production at home and abroad, together with a reasonable degree of profit.[29]

This may seem fair, but trade theory points to its obvious flaw: differences in costs of production are the very basis for trade, for comparative advantage. Tariffs destroy that basis.[30]

Such a political platform, mild as it is, leads only to more protection. It is a concession to foreigners, not an achievement for the nation's consumers. Mercantilist notions about national advantage interfere with clear thinking about comparative advantage.[31] They interfere with clear thinking about supply and demand, notably that if wages increase because they are protected, even if in only one industry so, too, will the price of goods and services—in *all* industries. The benefit cannot outweigh the cost.[32]

Politicians mislead a nation when they say that the imposition of tariffs raises domestic employment. It lowers exports. It leads to unemployment. See the following reports by the U.S. Department of Labor:

The Multilateral Approach to Trade Liberalization

Table 10-2. Trade and Employment Effects of Tariff Cuts in the Tokyo Round: Results for the United States When Trade Changes Are Balanced by Changes in Exchange Rates

Sectors	Change in Trade (in millions of dollars)			Change in Employment (in thousands of jobs)		
	Exports	Imports	Net	Exports	Imports	Net
All sectors	2,900	2,900	0	147.0	148.2	0.2
Primary agriculture	47	7	39	6.2	−2.9	3.3
Mining	−4	8	−12	1.5	−1.7	−0.2
Manufacturing	2,858	2,885	−27	92.6	−95.8	−3.2
Services	—	—	—	47.6	−47.8	−0.2

Source: U.S. Department of Labor, Bureau of International Labor Affairs, *Trade and Employment Effects of Tariff Reductions Agreed to in the MTN*, 1980, Table C.1. Employment changes in each sector include those induced by tariff cuts on products made by other sectors.

[33]

[Under Change in Trade, exports equal imports, 2,900 equals 2,900, because discrepancy is balanced by central bank borrowing (with interest paid by taxpayers). Under Change in Employment, discrepancy is balanced by employment elsewhere (or unemployment).]

Are these reports read by voters? No, which is why they are not mentioned by politicians. Arguing with voters who are losing their jobs is not how populist politicians win an election. On the contrary, they ask voters what they want—jobs—and just give it to them.[34]

But politicians should tell voters the truth (as before the signing of the North American Free Trade Agreement, in 1993, those on the Left did not), that free trade does not lead to a loss of jobs. Protecting jobs in defiance of economic theory is like not protecting the environment in defiance of ecological theory—why Brazilian and Indonesian politicians do not stop the cutting of rain forests—to create employment in farming.

Market reality (see economic truth) is that exports and imports adjust to each other: trade always balances. When a nation imports more than it exports, an exporting nation will then have so much of an importing nation's currency on hand that when it goes to sell that currency, i.e., convert it in order to pay its workers, supply of that currency will so far exceed its normal demand that its value will drop.

That's the balancing act. Exporting nations hold so much devalued currency that now their own profits and wages are devalued. So much so that they can no longer import products from other nations. [China and Japan do this perversely. They purposely devalue their *own* currency so that their exports are cheaper, and other nations' imports are more expensive. China and Japan sell to the world, yet buy nothing back—pure mercantilism (the counter argument of which is among the central premises of David Hume, *Political Discourses*, 1752, and Adam Smith, *The Wealth of Nations*, 1776—that government intervention distorts the natural market).]

And really, how smart is it for labor and capital both to be on the same side, to both want tariffs—to prevent foreign goods from entering the market? Trade policies that benefit one factor of production do not benefit the other. A trade policy that benefits labor does not benefit capital. For a country that produces capital-intensive goods such as automobiles, an increase in tariffs leads to an increase in price, but also to an increase in the real return to capital, which in turn is a reduction in the real return to labor—wages. If lower-priced foreign goods are kept out, workers are forced to pay $20,000 for a $15,000 automobile.[35] [This is one of the ways the price of goods and services currently outstrips the price of labor—see endnote *32*.]

In capital-intensive nations, owners of capital should favor protection of capital-intensive industries *regardless of the industry in which they personally are invested*. Workers, however, should oppose protection, *regardless of the industry in which they personally are employed*.

Trade is not optional human behavior. Trade is basic human nature playing out in the market. Only under totalitarian communism can such a force be eliminated.

Example: To get around U.S. quotas and tariffs, foreign automakers opened up factories in the U.S. In 1984, Toyota took over the NUMMI factory in Fremont, California (an inefficient General Motors plant where striking workers were actually sabotaging the plant), and agreed to hire all of them in exchange for *their* agreement to work in the "Japanese way"—where workers work as a team and contribute to quality control at every step of the way.

All of that is illusion. Except during periods of enormous economic expansion, union trade negotiators are no match for factory owners whose invested money is personally at risk. Toyota simply turned NUMMI into an assembly plant. It *looked* as if cars were being manufactured, but they were only being *assembled*. Workers there did work that any 12-year-old who loves building models can do, with increased automation that any video games player can do.

The same is true for parts. Japanese parts manufacturers opened up factories in the U.S. and hired workers but, again, only for low-end assembly work.

Thus, protection leads to distortion. And comes with a price. In the above example, the price was the *indirect* rise of Japanese imports. In general, however, the price of protecting industries, especially those in which a nation has the comparative advantage, is to lower the nation's standard of living. According to the 1990 study below, intervention caused consumer surplus in the U.S. to drop $70 billion, 1.3 percent of GDP. The study showed that the cost to the consumer of saving *a single job* from import competition often exceeded $500,000 *per year*—far more than the annual income of the worker whose job was protected.[36]

This is *the* case for free trade (and *the* case against socialism): protecting workers rather than producers leads to a lowering of the standard of living. The table below shows what it costs a nation to protect workers in particular industries:

The Evolution of Trade Policy

Table 10-3. Employment Effects of Tariff Cuts in the Tokyo Round: Detail for Selected U.S. Industries

Industry	Change in Number of Jobs			Net Change as Percentage of Industry Labor Force
	Exports	Imports	Net	
Office machinery	9,572	−2,345	7,227	2.25
Electrical components	11,793	−3,393	8,400	1.96
Aircraft and parts	10,158	−5,077	5,081	0.94
Electrical machinery	3,552	−1,609	1,943	0.43
Paper products	2,566	−1,086	1,480	0.31
Chemicals	2,762	−1,899	863	0.28
Metalworking machinery	2,920	−2,369	551	0.16
Printing and publishing	3,801	−2,066	1,735	0.16
Scientific instruments	3,160	−2,738	422	0.13
Misc. metal products	2,151	−2,664	−513	−0.10
Primary iron and steel	3,514	−4,585	−1,071	−0.12
Rubber and misc. plastics	1,781	−2,932	−1,151	−0.17
Electrical lights and wiring	2,281	−2,863	−582	−0.27
Lumber products	1,378	−2,973	−1,595	−0.27
Radio and TV equipment	3,771	−5,745	−1,978	−0.33
Apparel	698	−8,737	−8,039	−0.56
Fabrics, yarn, and thread	1,777	−5,303	−3,526	−0.60
Stone and clay products	791	−5,234	−4,452	−0.90
Miscellaneous manufacturing	2,010	−10,230	−8,220	−1.84

Source: U.S. Department of Labor, Bureau of International Labor Affairs, *Trade and Employment Effects of Tariff Reductions Agreed to in the MTN*, 1980, Tables C.2 and C.3 Industries listed are those in which the change due to exports or imports exceeds 2,500 jobs; employment changes in each industry include those induced by tariff cuts on products made by other industries.

[37]

In theory, some lost consumer surplus is recaptured by the tariff, but in practice that surplus does not find its way back to offset the cost. That is because nations that use tariffs also use other restraints, such as government imposed "voluntary export restraints, VERs."

To counter trade restraints, manufacturers in exporting nations look for innovative ways to cut production costs. Mainly they automate and eliminate workers. Yet citizens in importing nations also pay: tending not to change consumption habits, they continue to purchase imported goods, to pay the additional $5,000 for the imported automobile, to take money, thus, from their savings or to work extra hours.

———————

Tariffs and quotas also hurt developing nations. Why should rich nations spend money on foreign aid to help developing nations develop their industries (whose products are sold in the world market precisely because their own people are too poor to purchase them), and then not let those developing nations export their products duty free? Why even give foreign aid?

Laws against dumping also are misguided. Predatory pricing does not exist. Selling at a price less than it costs to produce—to drive weaker firms out of business, to create monopolies that will later raise prices—does not exist. Belief that it does is generated by populist politicians.

Consider a firm, even a monopoly, that sells its product in two markets and tries to maximize its long-run profits. The firm has a constant cost of production, the supply curve MC (because it has no control over the world price of commodities), yet in each market faces a different downward-sloping demand curve, AR. [Demand curves slope downward because demanders continue to purchase only if price drops—marginal utility theory.]

The firm's situation is shown in the three graphs below:

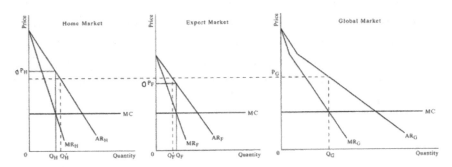

FIGURE 10-2
Dumping by a Firm with Monopoly Power
A firm has constant costs of production, so its marginal-cost curve is always *MC*. The firm has monopoly power in each market and will therefore maximize profits when its sales in that market equate marginal revenue with marginal cost. The panel on the left represents the firm's home market; the demand curve is AR_H, the marginal-revenue curve is MR_H, and the firm will sell OQ_H at the price OP_H. The center panel represents the firm's export market; the demand curve is AR_F, the marginal-revenue curve is MR_F, and the firm will sell OQ_F at the price OP_F. As OP_F is lower than OP_H, the firm will be dumping, even though it is not exporting at a loss to undercut foreign competitors. If forced to charge the same price in both markets, it will operate in the manner shown by the panel on the right. The curve AR_G is the (horizontal) sum of the home and foreign demand curves, and MR_G is the corresponding marginal-revenue curve. The firm will sell OQ_G and charge OP_G (it will sell OQ'_H in the home market and OQ'_F in the export market.) The price OP_G is below the profit-maximizing home price OP_H but above the profit-maximizing export price OP_F.

The firm's marginal-cost curve, MC, its supply curve, is the same in each market—the horizontal line. The demand curve in its home market is AR_H (average revenue, home). The demand curve shows total revenue (price times quantity) at every level of output as an average of all the firms in a nation producing the same product. The corresponding marginal-revenue curve is MR_H (the revenue from selling *one* more unit of output at any point on the demand curve). The point where the marginal revenue curve crosses the marginal cost curve is the output level at which firms maximizes profit—the reason for including a marginal revenue curve, in that producing lesser or greater output earns the firm less profit. The demand curve in its export market is AR_F (average revenue, foreign), and the marginal-revenue curve is MR_F.

Again, in each market the firm maximizes profit when marginal revenue from sales equals marginal cost of production, where MR crosses MC. Thus, the firm will sell OQ_H (monopoly quantity, home) in the home market [first graph] by setting its domestic price at OP_H, (monopoly price, home) and will sell OQ_F in the export market [second graph] by setting its export price at OP_F (which is lower than OP_H). The firm is not a predator. The prices OP_H and OP_F are long-run profit-maximizing prices set in different markets. Still, the firm is violating the first test in the GATT code (General Agreement on Trade and Tariffs), because its export price is lower than the price it charges normally in its home market.[38]

What would the firm do if it could not "dump" its product? It would add up its foreign and domestic demand curves to obtain the global demand curve AR_G and the corresponding global marginal-revenue curve MR_G [third graph]. It would then sell at OQ_G (global quantity) and charge OP_G (global price). But OP_G is higher than OP_F and lower than OP_H. In this instance, the rule *against* dumping has the odd effect of hurting the firm's foreign customers by helping its domestic customers.[39] Bravo! Not only does anti-dumping legislation cause price to drop in the *home* country, it causes output in the home country to increase, from QH to QH'. And because it caused price to rise for foreign buyers it caused output for foreign buyers to drop, from QF to QF'.

The cost of production test has an additional defect. It penalizes firms that lower their prices at a time when demand is temporarily depressed. Consider a firm that has high fixed costs of production typical of steel mills and other capital-intensive industries. When demand is repressed by a recession or events in the firm's industry, the firm may be unable to cover its full costs. It should not shut down, however, if it can cover its *variable* costs and have anything left over to meet some of its fixed costs. If it were to shut down completely, it would still have to cover its fixed costs (by borrowing or drawing down cash reserves). If it continues to operate, even at low prices, and can cover some of its fixed costs, it will minimize its losses. That, too, is considered dumping, because its export prices are lower than its total unit costs.[40]

The cost-of-production rule is frequently interpreted unfairly. Foreign firms are simply assumed to have higher fixed costs and profit margins than domestic firms. Hence, the cost-of-production rule will overstate the normal price in the foreign firms' domestic market and make it more likely that they will be charged with dumping. The rule against dumping has become a popular way for domestic firms to obtain protection against import competition.[41]

A prohibition against export subsidies was written into the original GATT. Governments that cut tariffs can expect other governments to do the same. They don't expect governments, then, to subsidize their own export industries. If the United States has a ten percent tariff on imported steel but Brazil gives a ten percent export subsidy to its steel industry, Brazilian steel will enter the United States at its free-trade price, and the American steel industry will not be protected. Widespread use of export subsidies undermines trade liberalization and leads to tariff warfare.[42]

3

MISCONCEPTIONS ABOUT WEALTH

Inequality of Income

Egalitarian economists doubt whether the market can distribute income and wealth fairly. They are correct because there is a trade-off between socially desirable income equality and market efficiency. "The market is generous to those who are successful in operating efficient enterprises that are responsive to consumer demand, and it is ruthless in penalizing those who are unable or unwilling to satisfy consumer demand efficiently."[1] However, this is far better than the reverse: inefficient markets with inefficient employment, where everyone is paid a day's wages for work that can be done in half a day—for the sake of equality.

"Creative destruction"—ruthless, continual—destroys firms, creates unemployment, yet keeps markets efficient, creates meaningful work. Not achieved in a socialist economy, where the only meaningful work is social work, work that does not attract creative entrepreneurs. How about a socialist-capitalist compromise? No! A nation half-controlled, half-free, does not work. Like those enslaved, controlled people do only minimal work. The near-compromise that we have today in Europe and America is satisfactory only to those who are not aware how much it really costs.[2]

Those who advocate income equality like to display the Lorenz curve, a curve which measures the percentage of a nation's total income as earned by various income classes. The Lorenz curve is divided into five income groups. In 1986, in the U.S., for example, the lowest fifth (lowest income earners) received 4.6% of the nation's income, while the highest fifth (highest earners) received 43.7% of the nation's income.[3] In 2011, the lowest fifth received less than 4% of the nation's income while the highest fifth's rose to 51.1%.[4] The Lorenz curve would be perfectly straight if each fifth earned exactly 20%, indicating equality of income:

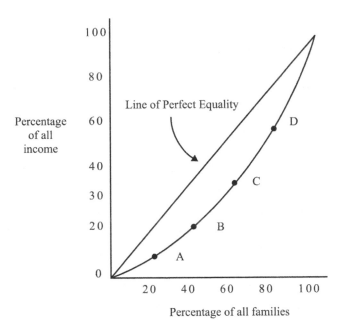

Equality of income *sounds* fair, yet it is a misleading guide for measuring social well-being. It uses value-laden terms that imply the ideal Lorenz curve is one that achieves perfect equality.[5]

Does a nation want perfect equality? If everyone earned the same amount, teachers would earn the same as doctors, miners would earn the same as teachers, but markets would be inefficient: socialism.

Socialism is not a justifiable ideal.[6] The only just distribution of income is one that pays individuals in relation to the demand for their labor. Best is to pay individuals relative to how much preparation went into the skill of their labor, but that is not how markets work. If everyone earned the same, there would be no incentive to excel, to invest, to take risk: there would be no reward. No one in Cuba, for example, with an idea for a product starts a company and hires people to work. It's illegal![7]

From an economic perspective, if an employer were to offer employees a percentage of the company's profit rather than a wage, labor unions (thinking they were protecting their members) would say that such an action is obscene, that an employee who works 40 hours a week and whose family is dependent upon his income should not have his wages subject to the success of the firm (even if that wage were twice as much). Yet that is why business owners sometimes earn tremendous salaries: they (and their families) are at risk. In the eighteenth century, the French economist Turbot (known by that one name) stated the trade-off for risk is that those who want immediate salary will get it at its present value, the discounted value of what its future value would have been had they waited.

Again, income inequality creates the incentive to earn more.[8] The Lorenz curve explains nothing. It does not explain why in some countries inequality leads to success and in others to failure. Nor does the Lorenz curve show an increase in a nation's standard of living. The curve does not show that the bottom fifth in the U.S. live better than the top fifth in much of the rest of the world.

Inequality is a nonissue laden with relative value. A graph that represents absolute value looks entirely different:[9]

FIGURE 15–4
Distribution of Household Income: United States, 1987

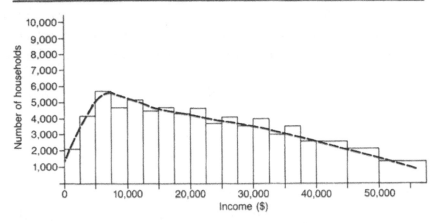

Source: U.S. Bureau of the Census, *Current Population Reports*, 1987.

Income levels are spread out fairly evenly. No need for redistribution. *What's important is that absolute income increase over time.* Shift the whole curve one inch to the right, and the number of poor households diminishes and the number of middle-class and wealthy increases. The country, however, is better off even if the top fifth has an enormous increase in income. What's important in an economy is that production continually rises, because as production rises, income rises, including that of the bottom fifth.

Not everyone believes this. Nobel Laureate Joseph Stiglitz believes that growing inequality in both opportunity and economic outcomes is the reason the U.S. economy [2013] is failing to recover from the 2008 financial crisis.[10] In 2009, unemployment rose to over 9.9 percent, and in most of 2013 was still nine percent, yet, according to Burton Abrams, a research fellow at the Bay Area's Independent Institute, inequalities in opportunity are as narrow today as they have ever been.[11] Why then is inequality in income even an issue, when, in fact, the U.S. economy provides more opportunity than any other nation, provides the highest standard of living, and provides high levels of entitlements?

Where, asks Abrams, is the plausible chain of causation between the phenomenon of inequality and the current economic stagnation?[12]

With respect to the slow economic recovery, perhaps it's uncertainty about regulation and taxation of the economy; about the Affordable Care Act (approved only because it was determined by the Supreme Court to be a *tax* and not a requirement for being a U.S. citizen); or the uncertainties with Dodd-Frank financial regulation. Perhaps it's due to the huge loss of household wealth that followed the popping of the real estate bubble.

Paul Krugman and other Keynesians suggest that we increase government expenditures to offset this loss of individual wealth. They are serious about this. Japan, for example, builds highways and bridges to nowhere; Keynes himself said that to get an economy going, employ people to dig holes and then let them refill them—liberal elitism at its worst.

Perhaps it is the extension of unemployment insurance to as long as 99 weeks that encourages people not to hurry back to work. Perhaps it's deficit spending and massive enlargement of an inefficient government sector that takes money away from the private sector.

What about our almost complete lack of national savings, which forces us to borrow from foreign countries (and pay them interest), keeping our exchange rate high, our exports less competitive (by raising demand for the dollar among those nations that loan them back to us—borrowed because our government spends more than it collects in revenue).

Perhaps the enormous expansion of the economy was a result of fraud—subprime mortgages and phony derivatives—that now requires an enormous period of recovery.

Inequality of outcome, per se, is not an issue. Inequality demonstrates that the economy is dynamic:

> A stagnant, equal-income Chinese society was converted into a dynamic growth machine precisely by allowing such inequality. Just try to imagine a Chinese economist

claiming that income inequality there is holding back the Chinese economy![13]

Compare with Professor Stiglitz's solution to inequality: "... significant investments in education, a more progressive tax system and a tax on financial speculation."

Stiglitz should mind his own business. As an economist, with respect to the economy's downturn, he might compare what happened before and after, but not make suggestions as to what to do during. When has a country ever taxed its way to prosperity? With taxes that no one pays, Greece and Argentina provide "free" education through the university level, but they would be better off if they didn't. In other words, public policy that recommends greater equality misses the big picture. The recommendations are counterproductive.

That alone is not a reason not to apply them. Political reality plays a part. Do we want a populist revolution? Do we want socialism? If not, preserving economic freedom requires handing out money whenever there is social unrest: it's the price of freedom. Still, short-term welfare is one thing; economic stimulus another. The Congressional Budget Office regularly reports that the results of the 2009 stimulus package were negative: there was no short-term increase in economic activity, and after 2016, GDP will be lower than it would have been had there been no stimulus, although the measure may have helped prevent financial collapse.[14]

For nations to correct a downturn in the economy, or a budget deficit, the proper course is to submit to a program of austerity—not to pretend that everything is okay. Has any country that committed to austerity been successful? It seems that Canada, Ireland, the Netherlands, and Finland have. Perhaps these governments are less afraid of a populist overthrow, or their citizens are more disciplined. Perhaps U.S. citizens are not, which is why we listen to populist economists such as Paul Krugman, who once stated (when no one was looking):

The point here is that the end of the Depression—which is the usual, indeed perhaps the sole, motivating example for the view that a one-time fiscal stimulus can produce sustained recovery, does not actually appear to fit the story line too well...[15]

In other words, Krugman did not get a Nobel Prize for his weekly Op-Ed column in the New York Times for which he is paid to write as a populist, but from a lifetime of work among economists, the vast majority of whom do not believe that government intervention can reverse a recession. [For a politician who believed and acted upon what she said, see Appendix E, Margaret Thatcher.]

The Asian Tigers

How was it possible that Japan and the four Tigers, Hong Kong, Taiwan, Singapore, and South Korea, rose literally from rags to riches in one generation—starting with the entire population at the bottom fifth—to a normal distribution along the Lorenz curve? It's an economic miracle unparalleled in modern industrial society. China is joining the club. Was it massive government aid?

Or, was it observing economic laws that suggest hard work, high rates of saving and investment, heavy dependence on export markets, and small but strong government? According to Skousen, it would be fundamentally wrong to credit the Tigers' success with insights of the Keynesian revolution that still overwhelm Europe and the U.S. in their reliance on partnership with government, and central planning.

Rather, according to Skousen:

...the remarkable success of the Pacific Basin countries is precisely due to their rejection of Keynesian and excessive central planning. These countries have done just the opposite of the Western nations, by taxing consumption at high rates through VATs, and taxation of savings at low rates. They have encouraged investment and capital formation by exempting most investment from taxation, while disencouraging consumption. In fact, credit cards and consumer loans are not in vogue in many parts of the Far East.

The belief that the newly industrialized economies are largely state-directed is a misinterpretation of history. The size of the government in each newly industrialized country remains relatively low compared to other industrialized nations, and the federal budget is usually balanced. Except for Hong Kong, they have all engaged in some form of industrial policy, but such activities have been more in the form of incentives than outright ownership and control, which has proven so disastrous in socialist countries. They all restructured their fiscal and monetary affairs, which provided a stable environment for economic growth and marketing, but final decision-making as to which investment areas to pursue was largely left to individual entrepreneurs.[16]

Besides following the same path, what Japan and the Tigers have in common is that none of them have resources. What nations that ask for foreign aid have in common is abundant resources, the "curse of resources." A curse, because nations with resources produce leaders who come to power promising to distribute the earnings—Hugo Chavez in Venezuela, rulers in the Middle East, socialist and populist politicians everywhere; they're like drug dealers who never let their addicted clients recover. The lesson from the Tigers is that foreign aid should be foreign investment. It should be investment in a nation's industry, not its government. It is not a coincidence that Britain and Holland are successful: neither has natural resources. It is not a fluke that Spain, having taken so much gold from the New World, during its entire history has been the poorest nation in Europe. According to Adam Smith in *Wealth of Nations*, it is because wealth is a function of production, not the stockpiling of gold. Stockpiling leads to inflation.

In 1986, the high savings rate in Japan represented 17.5 percent of disposable income compared to five percent in the U.S.[17] Unlike much of the Western world's savings which ended up in government securities, Japanese savings went to productive assets, to the stock market. In the 1980s, the Tokyo stock market was the largest in the world. The Asian Tiger model may not suit all cultures but in Japan the average worker puts in 60 hours a week, takes only three days of vacation a year, and maintains a culture of perfection on the production line; perhaps it's time for other cultures to consider that approach.[18] Perhaps the Mediterranean nations of Greece, Italy and Spain where the average workweek is 35 hours need a measure of austerity to grow their economies, eliminate their unfunded social security systems and their 26 percent unemployment rate among youth.

What about industries in Japan that did receive government assistance—from the Ministry of International Trade and Industry (MITI) and the Ministry of Finance? According to Skousen, those were some of Japan's major disappointments—ship building and the aerospace industry—both of which received government encouragement and funding. Yet those industries that were opposed by MITI, automobile and consumer manufacturing, were hugely successful. Other independent successful markets were cement, paper, glass and motorcycles. These received little assistance from MITI.[19]

The success of Japan and the Asian Tigers was not due to government industrial policy. It was due to savings, productive investments, work ethic, management skills, low taxes, and small stable governments. According to Skousen, those governments recognized their limitations. Even when governments intervene more than necessary, as in Singapore and South Korea but also in Germany, as long as government is pushing private industry to make the decisions, and citizens are living according to the above formula, nothing else is necessary.[20]

Redistribution of Income

The Communist Manifesto spells out ten points for a communist revolution:

- Abolish private property, and apply all rent from land to public purposes.
- Impose a heavily graduated income tax.
- Abolish all inheritance.
- Confiscate the property of all emigrants and rebels.
- Centralize all credit in the hands of the state.
- Centralize all means of communication and transport in the hands of the state.
- Place all factories and means of production in the hands of the state. Cultivate all land, including waste land.
- Ensure equal liability of all to labor (everyone must work). Establish industrial armies, especially for agriculture.
- Combine agriculture with manufacturing. Gradually abolish the distinction between town and country by redistributing the population over the entire country.[21]
- Institute free education for all children. Abolish child labor in its present forms. Combine education with industrial production.

Let a nation do these things (except education for children) and that nation will regress to the Middle Ages. Why? Because nations cannot do for citizens what citizens must do for themselves. Take that road, and you are back to serfdom. (See *The Road to Serfdom* by Nobel economist F. A. Hayek, the book *most responsible* for the fall of the Soviet Union.) Remove the incentive to excel, to innovate, to save, to invest, to take risk, by controlling an economy per the Communist Manifesto, so that individuals do not reap the true reward of their labor, and you create George

Orwell's *Animal Farm*, Ayn Rand's *Atlas Shrugged*. There are no examples of advanced industrialized nations becoming prosperous as the result of forced labor. The American South before the Civil War did not produce enough wealth to pay its workers. It should have switched to manufacturing or, as in China today, allowed agricultural workers to keep a portion of what they produced. That would have increased production. Had the South freed its slaves, its economy would have been far more prosperous. A slave economy cannot compete with a free economy.

Not everything Karl Marx said is wrong. But his economic theories are wrong:[22] (For further insight into the mind of Karl Marx, see Appendix F, Preface to "A Contribution to the Critique of Political Economy.") His most profound error was that profit is distributable. Profit doesn't exist. In a competitive economy it is reduced to zero. The high income of an entrepreneur or CEO is that of a professional athlete, a function of a contract in which income is tied to a percentage of revenue received. Their high income is not a function of the exploitation of labor. In a market economy, if an entrepreneur or CEO is not offered their market percentage, they will be approached by firms that will. This is the most natural, most important law of business and economics: price is a function of supply and demand. (See Chapter 2, "Timeless Rates of Return," entrepreneurial compensation, page 9.)

Another fundamental socialist error is that an economy can be controlled. Marx was correct in advocating complete totalitarian dictatorship of the proletariat: the only way to stop a free economy cold in its tracks. Anything less rather than control a market economy will simply cause it to operate less efficiently: control an economy, and money will not flow naturally.[23] Leave just one area unregulated, and all money will go there. During a financial crisis, investors will stop investing in businesses, real estate and stock, but not in currency markets. Economies may come to a standstill, but not international currency markets.[24]

Marx incorrectly thought that as capitalism progressed there would be a corresponding increase in poverty, oppression, enslavement, degeneration and exploitation. There has been overwhelming evidence to the contrary. As profit increases, so, too, do wages. Throughout the industrial revolution wages never dropped to subsistence.[25] The fact that workers do not earn as much as owners of business has nothing to do with exploitation, but with the fact that business owners are at risk, that business owners may never be paid the opportunity cost of their invested money. To redistribute money earned as a result of risk is to break all laws of money. Nor did Marx consider the time value of money. He was completely ignorant of the fact that workers' salaries are calculated as the discounted present value of what would have been their future income (had they waited to be paid until the final product was completed and sold). Why pretend this is not so? If nations want equality of income, let them create a communist economy—but be prepared for a drop in standard of living.[26]

Marxism does not work. Compare North Korea to South Korea, East Germany to West Germany. Look at Ghana. A rich country before independence, it turned to Marxism, and through price-control and state purchasing of monopolies, destroyed its entrepreneurial economy. Before 1960, Ghana was the world's leading producer of cocoa and a major exporter of gold. It took the road to serfdom and became exactly that, a nation in poverty.[27]

During its maturing process, communism wants to be international—at a minimum to prevent its citizens from comparing their economy to market economies. Socialist liberals who disparage the acquisition of material things forget that they live in a free society where it is wealth and protection of private property that create the base from which it is possible to express that rejection. It's not a coincidence (perhaps a necessity) that few socialist liberals ever lived in a communist country—not vacationed, but lived and worked—actually competed for basic necessities, experienced the boredom of life in a country where no one is entrepreneurial, where, as in France, those who operate even small businesses are mocked and ostracized.[28] Nor have most liberals ever manufactured or produced a product on a large scale.

42

They do not think from a business owner's perspective. They cannot.

It never occurs to liberals that a highly industrialized society, if collectivized, will fail. Here are the reasons why:

1. State planning separates costs from the users of a good or service (why health care in America is three times what it should be: government intervention has so distorted the market for health care that the market no longer exists—health insurance is no longer insurance but prepaid health care; consumers do not bargain price and service and insurance companies do not question the bill; they raise premiums—which employers pay because it increases their tax write-off, and government, Medicare, Medicaid, pays because government is out of control).

2. State monopolies lack competitive bidding (protected from competition, they raise prices for the purpose of paying for a nation's social security, health care and pensions—precisely how fascist governments come to power: they create the corporate state in order to promise and pay for all of the above).

3. A corporate state or a communist state eliminates competition (meaning that firms then have no way to know how much to charge, except to employ Marxist labor theory of value, i.e., add up the hours used to make a product and then guess at a price (meaning copy prices in the West), thus eliminate price determined as a function of supply and demand, why the centrally dictated Soviet Union generated chronic surpluses and shortages.[29]

4. An economy in which billions of interpersonal transactions take place every second of the day is too complex and interrelated to be commanded.

5. State-run industries do not innovate (in that a government-controlled factory is not a creative environment), nor does it reward creativity.

[A reoccurring theme of this book is that redistribution, as under progressive taxation, always means from the middle class to the poor. The rich contribute something, but hardly notice the perversely regressive tax. A curious feature of the Chinese economy is that while migrant workers live in overcrowded dormitories, apartments remain empty. Landlords view them as stores of value, not as sources of rent. Does socialist China have an obligation to redistribute such housing?[30]

Interfering with the market only makes people worse off. If simply writing a check to those in need would solve the problem, that might be an option, but not one that addresses the real problem: economic growth—the real solution to poverty.[31] Here is an excellent statement:

> Of the tendencies that are harmful to sound economics, the most seductive, and in my opinion the most poisonous, is to focus on questions of distribution. In this very minute, a child is being born to an American family and another child, equally valued by God, is being born to a family in India. The resources of all kinds that will be at the disposal of this new American will be on the order of 15 times the resources available to his Indian brother. This seems to us a terrible wrong, justifying direct corrective action, and perhaps some actions of this kind can and should be taken. But of the vast increase in the well-being of hundreds of millions of people that has occurred in the 200-year course of the industrial revolution to date, virtually none of it can be attributed to the direct redistribution of resources from rich to poor.

The potential for improving the lives of poor people by finding different ways of distributing current production is *nothing* compared to the apparently limitless potential of increasing production."

—Nobel Laureate Robert Lucas[32]

Flat Tax

The only fair tax is a flat tax: Everyone pays the same rate.

Unfair is a progressive tax: the wealthy pay at a higher rate than the poor.[33]

Why do nations even have taxation? For defense: against foreign invasion, against civil unrest. Taxation is the cost of ensuring safety and order, the cost of living in a civil society. In the West, it is the price of freedom, insurance against populism, against demagogues and corrupt politicians (Juan Peron, Hugo Chavez, Adolph Hitler, Tammany Hall) who rile the masses with promises of goods, services, even jobs, paying them off in exchange for their vote.[34]

There are, then, two groups in this world—those who get back in spending more than they pay in total tax (in a sense being paid to go away), and those who pay more in taxes than they get back in spending, for example, working parents who pay taxes, then pay again to send their children to private schools because public schools aren't good enough. In the U.S., $1.5 trillion in income is redistributed from to the top 40 percent to the bottom 60 percent.[35]

The rationale is economic justice. However, more important is economic growth. The graph below shows that even if social and economic growth are at times driven by taxation, in the U.S., our attempt to extract every possible dollar to satisfy every possible public need has gone too far.

Tax Complexity Keeps Piling Up

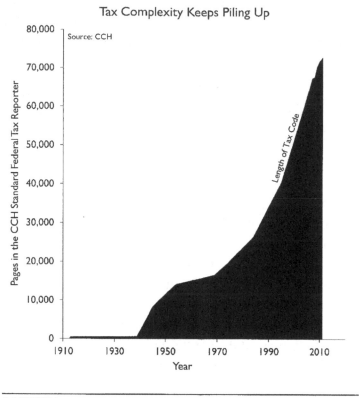

Source: CCH

Length of Tax Code

Pages in the CCH Standard Federal Tax Reporter

(x-axis) Year: 1910, 1930, 1950, 1970, 1990, 2010

(y-axis) 0, 10,000, 20,000, 30,000, 40,000, 50,000, 60,000, 70,000, 80,000

36

The tax code has made the Internal Revenue Service (IRS) a super-agency that duplicates the work of every other cabinet agency, from Energy and Education to Health and Human Services (HHS) and Housing and Urban Development (HUD). Were we to start from scratch, we would not let a tax collection agency perform these functions. Tax reform *is* necessary.[37]

The central argument in tax debates in Washington, unfortunately, is not about efficiency or economic growth, but about the distribution of taxes—which income groups should pay more or less of the tax burden. This problem is compounded by the fact that progressive taxation is only half the picture. Progressive taxation can, in fact, also be achieved through spending. If we moved to a flatter, more neutral tax code to lower the tax burden on upper-income families, an overall balance of progressivity could be maintained by cutting the types of federal spending that benefit high-income families.[38]

Interestingly, the amount of federal spending that families of various income levels receive is not all that different. What differs is the amount of federal taxes they pay. In the graph below, note that even households that earned $37,000 to $67,000 received more in federal spending than they paid in federal taxes.

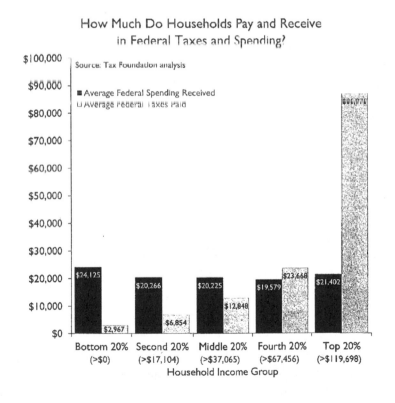

How Much Do Households Pay and Receive
in Federal Taxes and Spending?

Source: Tax Foundation analysis

- Average Federal Spending Received
- Average Federal Taxes Paid

$100,000
$90,000
$80,000
$70,000
$60,000
$50,000
$40,000
$30,000
$20,000
$10,000
$0

Bottom 20%   Second 20%   Middle 20%   Fourth 20%   Top 20%
(>$0)   (>$17,104)   (>$37,065)   (>$67,456)   (>$119,698)

Household Income Group

$24,125 $2,967
$20,266 $6,854
$20,225 $12,848
$19,579 $23,668
$21,402 $86,978

Those who want tax reform argue that both taxes and spending should be lowered. No one is arguing that there should be no redistribution. Those who suggest that corporate tax rates should be higher are making an enormous mistake: American corporations are already the highest taxed in the world. See graph below.

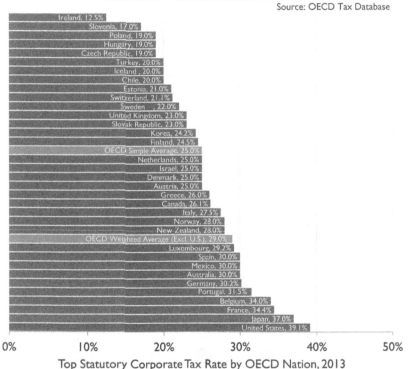

The U.S. Has the Highest Corporate Income Tax Rate in the Industrialized World

Source: OECD Tax Database

Top Statutory Corporate Tax Rate by OECD Nation, 2013

40

The biggest tax loopholes go to individuals: deductibility for mortgage interest on owner-occupied homes (yet, also commercial real estate); deductibility for pensions and employee benefits such as a 401(k); and for exclusion of employer-provided health insurance. See graph below:

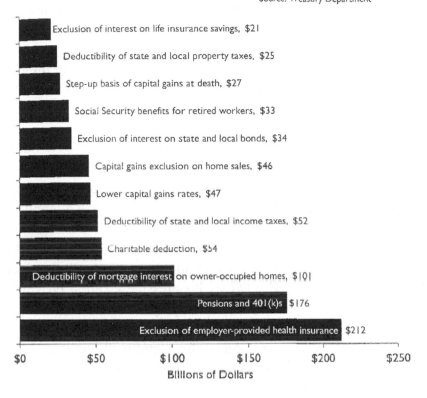

The Dozen Largest Individual Tax Preferences in 2014
Source: Treasury Department

- Exclusion of interest on life insurance savings, $21
- Deductibility of state and local property taxes, $25
- Step-up basis of capital gains at death, $27
- Social Security benefits for retired workers, $33
- Exclusion of interest on state and local bonds, $34
- Capital gains exclusion on home sales, $46
- Lower capital gains rates, $47
- Deductibility of state and local income taxes, $52
- Charitable deduction, $54
- Deductibility of mortgage interest on owner-occupied homes, $101
- Pensions and 401(k)s $176
- Exclusion of employer-provided health insurance $212

$0 $50 $100 $150 $200 $250

Billions of Dollars

41

In 2011, 54 million federal income tax filers had no income tax liability. In 2009, 58 million. The question is: should the above loopholes be closed or expanded? If closed, middle income families, mostly baby boomers nearing retirement—the largest, best educated and highest paying group—will end up paying most of the nation's taxes.

Should tax reform really be about transferring the payment of taxes from one group to another? Why is it wrong to lower or even eliminate taxes when we know that doing so would lead to economic growth—to a higher standard of living, more jobs, higher wages, greater economic opportunity? The Tax Foundation estimates that if top individual and corporate tax rates were lowered to 25 percent, GDP would rise by over 4.7 percent, investment in plant and equipment by 11.53 percent, and productivity, which translates to wages, nearly three percent.[42]

Because it's not as simple as that. Lowering taxes or imposing a flat tax, especially at 25 percent, which is high for a flat tax, implies *not* eliminating tax loopholes. Those loopholes exist precisely as concessions by government to encourage investment and to prevent double taxation.[43]

Interest paid on a mortgage is a tax deduction (to encourage home ownership)—except that interest is also taxed as income to the lender. Shouldn't it be one or the other? Deposits to 401(k)s, to pensions, are subtracted from gross income before calculating tax, although taxed later when distributed at retirement.

Capital gain taxes are paid by the corporation, yet when capital gains are distributed to individual investors, stockholders, they are taxed again. Why twice? Progressive taxation provides a loophole for multi-year income averaging—to prevent unfairness to those whose income fluctuates, for example, a salesperson who works three years to close a deal, who is not paid one-third of the commission each year, which would be taxed at 30 percent, but is paid in full in year three, which is taxed at 50 percent.

Tax loopholes exist also to encourage donation to charity.

A flat tax of 15 percent, according to advocates such as Steve Forbes, would eliminate these loopholes:

1. There would be no tax on Social Security, no tax on pensions, no tax on personal savings. Capital gains tax would be reduced. A family of four would pay no tax on the first $36,000 of income.[44]

2. Everyone would pay the same rate. Like a sales tax, a flat tax is proportional to the amount of money spent, not to the wealth of the purchaser.

In a progressive system, the higher the bracket, the higher the rate. In a regressive system, the higher the bracket, the lower the rate. A flat tax, then, is not regressive.[45] The term "progressive" sounds as though it means something good, something liberals would advocate, and "regressive" sounds like something bad, but both terms are simply descriptions of two sorts of graduated taxes: one in which rates rise (progress) with income, and one in which they fall (regress).[46]

3. Problems with distribution and allocation of tax revenue would be resolved by a flat tax. With no marginal rates, with no change in tax rate as one changes income bracket, provided the tax rate is low, simply an insurance premium for living in a free and civil society, there would not be enough revenue to fight over. *That* would eliminate the kind of political debate in the U.S. that shuts down government every time there is disagreement over taxation.

4. Even if the *average* rate for a progressive tax rate system is the same as a flat tax, the progressive rate system is less efficient. This is true from the perspective of the optimal rate: zero. Those in higher brackets who pay out more in taxes than they receive plus pay higher proportionally, currently are forced to make a trade-off between working more and paying a higher proportion in taxes, or working less and paying a lower proportion in taxes. A flat tax rate closer to zero allows them to work more, earn more, and not worry about the tax.

5. The argument in favor of progressive taxation, of wealth redistribution, is that poverty, even when imagined, cannot be ignored.[47] If to a poor person one dollar is worth more than it is to a rich person,

then a tax system that shifts more of the tax burden onto the rich would produce a net benefit to society.[48] [If one dollar has lower marginal utility to the rich, then taxing the rich at a higher rate is not unfair.][49]

It should, in fact, be the basis for progressive taxation: marginal utility. Tax citizens at the rate they can live with.

––––––––––

Market reality and human nature underlie the above arguments—and lead to another conclusion.

Lack of competition explains lack of growth before the Industrial Revolution. Pre-1700 there was little taxation and regulation, yet no growth. Today there is excessive taxation and regulation, yet enormous growth.

In pre-industrial economies, wealth flowed up from the bottom of society to the top (as taxes and exploitation of labor), and stayed there. In democratic societies, capitalist economies, wealth is created by everyone, plus progressive taxation makes wealth flow back down (helps it to circulate), but the poor have inherent problems that "progressives" are reluctant to acknowledge, believing that the problems of the poor are not their fault, that they would disappear in a utopian world without competition—pre-Industrial Revolution. The inherent problem of the poor is that those who do not know how to make money don't know how to keep it—it's why the poor have debt, why they mortgage whatever they own, why they constantly transfer wealth back to the rich.

Plus, after the 2008 financial crash, to encourage economic growth—more borrowing, more home loans, more quantitative easing—central banks increased the money supply. But, banks hoarded the money. When pressured to make loans, they simply called their best customers, those with absolutely no need to borrow, and begged them to borrow. Money rarely went to those who needed it, homeowners. Quantitative easing did give banks the confidence they needed, but it also contributed, in 2014, to a rise in the price of real estate and stocks back to their 2007 level—again, a rise in value of the assets of the wealthy.

Investment Analysis

The very purpose of negotiation for the purchase of an asset is to move the party with the asset to sign a contract to transfer it.[50] For the acquirer, that is the start of wealth creation.

That act of signing, a physical act, an emotional act where parties take pen in hand and sign their names is itself not necessarily the product of an act of reasoning. Rational analysis, the key to deciding *to* invest, is not the key to deciding *which* investment. Timing is the key to that decision.

If they thought this way, business schools couldn't exist. Business schools need to teach something, so they teach comparative investment analysis, how, for example, to calculate an internal rate of return. The underlying assumption is that there is always more than one investment to choose from, and that variables such as income and expense are known quantities.

Both assumptions are false. Rarely are purchasers offered more than one viable project at a time; rarely is an income-and-expense statement other than a projection; rarely do purchasers choose investments as a result of comparing internal rates of return.[51]

In reality most asset purchasers are "price takers," lucky even to be offered an investment. However, professional investors, like trained athletes, are not price takers; they are price makers. With professional investment, deals are made, not found.

Still, long term, amateur or professional, neither can avoid a fundamental economic truth—that real rates of return are timeless: one percent on savings, two to three percent on mortgage lending, three to five percent on venture capital. A rate that is higher is not a rate; it's not profit; it's entrepreneurial compensation.

———————

Economics is about trade-offs, about actions at a moment in time, about opportunity costs. Economics is a reminder that there are consequences to every action. Differences in interest rates are a warning as to just how serious those consequences can be—that when rates are higher than their timeless rate, something is wrong.[52]

Rates much higher than their timeless rate indicate that something is terribly wrong. Economists say that rates are determined in the market through the interplay of the supply and demand for money, but that's not always true. In the short run, interest rates are determined by central banks; only in the long run are they timeless. Rates that are higher are accounting for inflation and/or risk, for the probability that money lent may earn less than the expected interest, or be lost altogether. Fear of project failure, market collapse, nationalization of industries, these are reasons why lenders raise their rates from five to ten percent, why sovereign debt bonds can rise to 20 percent.

———————

What is an internal rate of return? It is a return that factors over a period of time all sources of income and expense, including the cost of borrowing. If that rate is zero there is no benefit, no value to the project: dollars spent are offset by dollars earned. A dollar in hand is better employed deposited in a bank to earn one percent interest, or lent for a mortgage to earn two percent, or used as venture capital to earn five percent.

A dollar today is more valuable than a promise to pay a dollar one year from now: the dollar today can be invested to grow by a factor of $(1+r)$. If interest, r, is 5 percent, then $1+r = \$1 + .05 = \$1.05$. Thus, the promise to receive $1.00 one year from now is worth $0.95 today (or the promise to receive $0.95 today is worth $1.00 one year from now). The present value formula is shown below:

$$\text{Present value of } \$1.00 \text{ in n years} = \$1(1+r)^n$$

Everyone should memorize the fact, if not the formula, that as either the interest rate, r, or number of years, n, increases, the discount rate diminishes. A dollar earning five percent interest is worth $1.05 at the end of one year. Multiplying that future value by the discount rate of 0.9524— using the present value formula— gives you its present value of $1.00. Not to think in these terms, not to discount a desired future value back to its present value, is what leads to ridiculous solutions to world problems.

For an everyday example, consider the following question:

A persistent life insurance salesman makes the following pitch: "At your age (40) a $100,000 whole life policy is a much better buy than a term policy. The whole life policy requires you to pay $2,000 per year for the next four years, but nothing after that. A term policy will cost you $400 per year for as long as you own it. Let's assume you live 35 more years—which means you'll end up paying $8,000 for the whole life policy and $14,000 for the term policy."

Which policy should you choose? You don't know until you have an interest rate. If the insurance company calculates that the premiums you pay earn five percent interest per annum, the company, using the present value formula, will tell you (but only if you ask, because they're trying to sell you the most expensive policy) the present value of the whole life policy (the one with $8,000 in payments) is $82,227: $100,000 multiplied by the discount rate of 0.8227, calculated from the formula as $100,000/$(1.05)^4$. Present value of the term policy (the one with $14,000 in payments) is $10,835: $100,000 multiplied by the discount rate of 0.1812, calculated as $100,000/(1.05)^{35}$. Determined this way, the whole life policy has a greater present value.

But, if the term policy offered an interest rate of one percent (because the insurance company calculates that it will earn only one percent on your premiums, perhaps because the amount paid annually is so little), then present value would be $70,590: $100,000 multiplied by the discount rate 0.7059 [$100,000/(1.01)^4$. Now the choice between life or term policies is less obvious.

Without knowing the interest rate, and without knowing that the higher the rate or the longer the time period for payments the greater the discount rate, there is no way to determine the present value of *anything*. The following examples show that as the rate in the denominator increases (or the number of years), dividing it into 1 (or $1) creates ever lower discount rates:

One percent interest for four years,

$$\text{Present value} = \frac{1}{(1.01)^4} = \frac{1}{1.01} \times \frac{1}{1.01} \times \frac{1}{1.01} \times \frac{1}{1.01} = 0.9609$$

Five percent interest for four years,

$$\text{Present value} = \frac{1}{(1.05)^4} = \frac{1}{1.05} \times \frac{1}{1.05} \times \frac{1}{1.05} \times \frac{1}{1.05} = 0.8227$$

10 percent interest for four years,

$$\text{Present value} = \frac{1}{(1.10)^4} = \frac{1}{1.10} \times \frac{1}{1.10} \times \frac{1}{1.10} \times \frac{1}{1.10} = 0.6830$$

One percent interest for 35 years,

$$\text{Present value} = \frac{1}{(1.01)^{35}} = \frac{1}{1.01} \times \frac{1}{1.01} \times \ldots \frac{1}{1.01} = 0.7059$$

Five percent interest for 35 years,

$$\text{Present value} = \frac{1}{(1.05)^{35}} = \frac{1}{1.05} \times \frac{1}{1.05} \times \ldots \frac{1}{1.05} = 0.1812$$

———

If you plan to borrow against your life insurance policy or later sell it, the policy you want is the one with the highest present value. This way of thinking applies also to solving world problems, global warming, for example. The *Stern Report*, 2006, commissioned by the United Nations, declares that there is no time to lose. Nations should chip in one percent of their GDP *per annum* to avoid a natural disaster which will be on a par with catastrophes associated with the great wars and economic depressions of the twentieth century. The *Stern Report* would have the world's economies cut back production now to have a better world in the future.[53]

Without a discount rate, there is no way to know if the *Stern Report* is correct. If the world believes that it's important to spend money today to prevent global warming in the future, then a low discount rate should be used. A low rate will make present generations acutely aware of how much they need to invest, now, to ensure a carbon-free environment in the future.

Because we do value the welfare of future generations, are we thus ethically bound to employ a low discount rate? Is that why the *Stern Report* advocates a near-zero discount rate—to emphasize intergenerational equity?

This panic approach of using a near-zero rate contrasts dramatically with use of a market rate that considers the opportunity costs of money (which at a low rate would actually kill off humanity). We might spend $52 billion today to save the environment 100 years from now, but should we spend $5.2 trillion today if in reality the cost to save the environment is $100 trillion? According to the *Stern Report*, it's not a question of gradually changing to cleaner production methods; it's a question of *immediately* changing to cleaner production methods. The world must not let cost be an issue: a near-zero discount rate *is* the correct rate. For a benefit of $100 trillion 100 years from now with a discount rate of one percent, the cost today would be $37 trillion.

$$\text{Present value} \;=\; \frac{\$100 \text{ trillion}}{(1+.01)^{100}} \;=\; \$37 \text{ trillion}$$

Because of the time value of money, a near-zero discount rate doesn't exist (which would reflect that money has no value). The world can forget about the *Stern Report*.

Yet the UN Intergovernmental Panel on Climate Change uses the *Stern Report* to calculate different scenarios for mean welfare per capita both for industrialized and developing nations, both with and without global warming, to compare years 2100 and 2200 to 1990. Between 1990 and 2100 the maximum cost of climate change for developing nations in their A1F1 category (upper-tier nations) is $5,000 per capita, and between 1990 and 2200, $46,800 per capita. For industrialized nations the cost is $8,000 and $75,000 respectively. See Table 1 and Table 2 on page 59:[54]

For a multi-trillion-dollar benefit to be received 200 years from now, perhaps the industrialized world would pay $8,000 per capita, but would not pay $75,000 per capita. The UN has no right to ask the industrialized world to pay such a premium for a scenario that may not even occur 200 years from now. Such a demand, besides ignoring standard economic analysis, ignores the prospects of new technology. And it ignores the capacity of humans to adapt. Why would Russians object to their tundra opening up for oil drilling and waterskiing? And why shouldn't we turn our backs on Al Gore, the Kyoto Protocols, and the Stern Report if the nature of progress is that future generations benefit from technological advances made today? We should reject the use of a zero discount rate and acknowledge that future generations will be wealthier and more technologically advanced. They, too, should pay part of the bill.

Table 1

Life Without Global Warming

Mean welfare per capita in the absence of climate change in the 1990 and 2100 for developing and industrialized countries, measured as GDP per capita (1990 U.S. dollars) per the IPCC sencarios.

Scenario	1990 Actual	2100 A1FI	A2	B2	B1
Developing countries	$900	$66,500	$11,000	$18,000	$40,200
Industrialized countries	$13,700	$107,300	$46,200	$54,400	$72,800
Global temperature increase, 1990-2085	N/A	4.0°C	3.3°C	2.4°C	2.1°C

SOURCES: *Arnell et al (2004), IPCC (2000)*

Table 2

The Costs of Warming

Mean welfare per capita in 2100 and 2200 for developing and industrialized countries, adjusting for the costs of climate change from m market effects, non-market (i.e., environmental and public health) effects, and the risk of cf catastrophe, per the *Stern Review's* 95the percentile estimate of costs.

A.

Scenario	1990 Antual	2100 A1FI	A2	B2	B1
DEVELOPING COUNTRIES					
GDPO per capita, no climate change	$900	$66,500	$11,000	$18,000	$40,200
Maximum cost of climate change	0	$5,000	$600	$500	$800
Net welfare per capita, with climate change	$900	$61,500	$10,400	$17,500	$39,400
INDUSTRIALIZED COUNTRIES					
GDPO per capita, no climate change	$13,700	$107,300	$46,200	$54,400	$72,800
Maximum cost of climate change	0	$8,000	$2,400	$1,500	$1,500
Net welfare per capita, with climate change	$13,700	$99,300	$43,800	$52,900	$71,300

B.

Scenario	1990 Actual	2200 A1FI	A2	B2	B1
DEVELOPING COUNTRIES					
GDPO per capita, no climate change	$900	$133,000	$22,000	$36,000	$80,400
Maximum cost of climate change	0	$46,800	$5,300	$4,500	$7,600
Net welfare per capita, with climate change	$900	$86,200	$16,700	$31,500	$72,800
INDUSTRIALIZED COUNTRIES					
GDPO per capita, no climate change	$13,700	$214,600	$92,400	$108,800	$145,600
Maximum cost of climate change	0	$75,500	$22,100	$13,700	$13,800
Net welfare per capita, with climate change	$13,700	$139,100	$70,300	$95,100	$131,800

SOURCES: *Author's calculations, based on Warren et al. (2006), Arnell et al. (2004), Stern Review, and World Bank data*

4

CONCLUSION

Prologue

Everything in life is interconnected. All human action, all laws of business and economics have a social, political and economic consequence. No human act is devoid of conflict.

To paraphrase Hegel, everything includes within itself the seeds of its own destruction. So, why not take a Zen approach and combine all the conflict: combine Western thought—the idea that social, political and economic rights of the individual *precede* those of the state—with Eastern thought—the idea that individual well-being co-exists *with* the state, that life is about reconciliation of opposites, freedom with responsibility, material with spiritual— and create the perfect society—a society where everyone takes responsibility for their own actions (and agrees not to hurt anyone else—not purposely commit a tort), and where government provides a single service: protection of life, liberty and property (which, in a market otherwise free of government intervention, would cause the price of all goods and services to drop by half).

Is this possible? It's what the creators of the U.S. Constitution had in mind.[1]

The three sections that follow, "Basic Laws of Business and Economics," "Basic Laws of Government" and "Basic Myths about the Economy," describe some of the natural forces underlying social, political and economic activity. Accompanying examples show that government intervention in the free markets of human association destroys those markets and makes life more expensive.

Basic Laws of Business and Economics

1. All economic activity is exchange:

Parties trade what they have in surplus, and by so doing raise their standard of living.

In this sense, trade is personal, between two parties. But the underlying variables of trade—price, supply, demand—are impersonal elements of doing business and operate globally. The price of oil is not a function of its domestic supply and demand; it is a function of world supply and demand and of world supply and demand for money.[2]

2. Every good and service has a single worldwide
    price:

That is the "law of one price." Factor in exchange rates and a McDonald's hamburger costs the same everywhere, China, France, the U.S.: the law of "purchase price parity."

A difference in price anywhere, therefore, is temporary, a signal that there is interference in the market.[3] A difference in price that reflects genuine difference in manufacturing processes, productivity or comparative advantage between nations is really a difference in profit level. This makes trade possible, leads to survival of only the most efficient firms, and is why the competitive process leads to a lowest single price. Eliminate genuine differences, protect a particular industry or a particular currency, boost exports at the expense of imports, accumulate gold or currencies—mercantilism—and nations which trade with each other will all experience inflation. At first, producers will pay the higher price for intermediate production inputs (at times a large percentage of a nation's imports), and raise the price of their final product (the nation's exports); eventually, with resource prices too high, less efficient firms are forced out of business (and their employees out of work), and the entire nation will be forced to pay artificially high prices for *all* goods and services.[4]

3. There is at least one unseen consequence for every
   act of interference in the economy:

We see the new baseball stadium. We do not see, however, the clothing store (and other businesses) that went out of business because the tax to pay for the stadium caused customers not to purchase what they might have otherwise, new clothing.

We see Social Security and Medicare as insurance for old age. We do not see that they are paid for by borrowing—that the bulk of the U.S. budget deficit is Social Security and Medicare—and that the borrowing takes money away from where it would go ordinarily.[5]

What will the trade-off be for the U.S. budget deficit—bankruptcy, increased taxation, cuts in government spending, a rise in contributions to Social Security, a rise in retirement age, means testing for Medicare?[6]

With government or union intervention in the economy to support wages or a struggling industry, we see specific jobs protected. We do not see, however, that protection of uncompetitive industry forces consumers to pay artificially higher prices not only for domestic products but with tariffs, also, for imports. To the extent imports exceed exports, there is a balance of payments problem.

The unseen consequence of a balance-of-payments problem is a forced devaluation of the nation's currency. Central banks then raise interest rates on government bonds to guarantee that foreign investors continue to buy those bonds (which pay the interest on but also fund the national deficit). The unseen price for raising the interest rate is that it leads to inflation, thus, destruction of the nation's currency, destruction of money invested in savings (see retirees) and creation of *artificially* high prices for stocks and real estate—another bubble, which when it bursts, is the start of the next recession.[7]

The worst trade-off in a budget deficit is that it puts a nation at risk of defaulting on its sovereign debt. In 476, Rome had so much debt it could no longer pay its military. With the Roman Empire defenseless, barbarians walked in unopposed and destroyed it.[8]

Moreover, nations that default on their debt cause others to default, even when those nations have no debt. According to Peter Kenen, an international trade economist, the IMF bailed out Malaysia, Singapore and Indonesia during the 1997-1998 Asian Crisis precisely because those nations did not have huge budget deficits, thus, *could* devalue their currencies and keep their exports competitive [something Greece cannot do because Greece no longer has its own currency].[9]

That devaluation led to a speculative attack on the Hong Kong dollar, which in turn drove up interest rates, provoking a precipitous fall in the Hong Kong stock market. The Asian crisis spread north to Korea. The decline in Hong Kong stock prices reverberated through the interconnected world's economies to New York. The Dow-Jones index fell by more than seven percent in a single day, even further on Latin American markets.[10]

Prices of raw materials then dropped. Russia, which lives off its raw materials, was deeply affected. Without profit from oil exports (coupled to no attempt at reforming its economy), Russia experienced capital flight and a weakened ruble. Its central bank was forced to raise short-term interest rates—by extension, the nation's budget deficit. Russia requested a bailout from the IMF— *which complied*, because Russia, according to Kenen, seemed too important to fail in political terms and too big to fail in economic terms.

Thailand, Indonesia and Korea also sought help from the IMF. The IMF acted, but required all three to keep interest rates high, preventing further currency depreciation which would have wiped out foreign investors.

The Asia Crisis was more severe than anyone realized: millions of workers lost their jobs, and huge numbers of families slipped into poverty. The crisis was so contagious it affected every country in the region, including Japan, which experienced a deep recession. As a result of the devalued currencies and high interest rates, businesses and banks became insolvent. Economies imploded.[11]

This is the real risk of a budget deficit. Sovereign debt default. Central banks increase interest rates to protect their nations' currencies. Production slows, unemployment rises, foreign and domestic investors pull back. Inflation will follow, annihilating a nation's savings, tempting weaker nations to peg their exchange rates to a stronger currency, which makes their currencies appear stronger and enables those nations to postpone dealing with their underlying problems.[12]

Inflation is bad because it sends a false signal to the market, a false price rise. The false price rise encourages firms to expand production as if there were an increase in demand when, in fact, there is only an increase in price. This triggers capital flight (as in response to an armed revolution) that leads to even more distortion, all told, to swings in prices, exports, imports, money supply, and unemployment (which really *is* cause for revolution).

[Perhaps the most profound problem with government regulation of an economy is that it creates investment decisions driven by regulation or tax considerations rather than by a project's inherent economic merit. In the long run, such projects, unsustainable, lead to economic collapse—another reason why nations are better off not taxing business and investment.]

4. Bond markets control a nation:

If nations deviate from sound economic practices, they will be punished by bond markets. Excessive government spending, as it translates into excessive economic growth and inflation, will be countered by high interest rates, thus, lower bond prices. Anyone who has to sell bonds, individuals or pension funds, will sell them at a loss.

Famously, when Bill Clinton first came to office as president and declared with joy that there was so much he could and would do for the country, he was told by his economic advisors, "No you won't!" In a complete turnaround from campaign promises, Clinton drastically reformed and cut the nation's welfare system. Why? The debt used to pay for it was destroying the bond market.

In other words, it was not national leaders, Germany's Angela Merkel, for example, who, during the euro crisis, pushed austerity on to Italy, Spain, Greece and others. Beginning in 2011, it was private lenders who declined to finance further borrowing by those countries. They stopped financing portions of their banking systems. It was markets, not political leaders, that triggered the eurozone crisis. According to Roger Altman, a former U.S. deputy treasury secretary, the fiscal and banking restructuring that follows is the price of rebuilding market confidence.[13]

The private sector, then, controls an economy. Investors, producers, consumers, it is they, not government, who make markets, who buy and sell goods and services, who buy and sell money. Twenty-first-century markets are more powerful than any government leader. A sovereign nation (or its banking system) that loses access to financing is fundamentally insolvent. Central banks, the IMF, the European Financial Stability Facility, such agencies can provide relief, even bailout, but their terms are identical to that of the market—a rate of return so high it can be paid only by a nation submitting to an unwanted regimen of austerity, reducing government support for social entitlements, and perhaps its national defense.[14]

    5. Economic efficiency is the basis for economic
       decisions.

To allow inefficiency is to accept lower production, lower economic growth, and a lower standard of living.

Economic efficiency is substantiated by the Efficient Market Hypothesis, by the notion that rates of return are timeless, and that in the long run, profit is zero. Cost-benefit analysis substantiates the importance of economic efficiency. It exposes citizens to economic reality, namely, that government intervention in an economy is expensive, citizens lose more than they gain, and intervention changes the direction in which money would naturally flow, all inefficiencies that reduce economic growth and standard of living.[15]

Basic Laws of Government

1. The purpose of government:

As stated in the Declaration of Independence, the purpose of government is to protect the natural right of all persons to their own life, liberty and property.[16] Stated also is that if government should stray from that purpose, citizens should abolish it.

Natural rights are the key. Nature. Organisms thriving on earth for a billion years without direction other than what's encoded in their DNA. It took modern man 200,000 years, his entire existence, to figure this out. Adam Smith, in 1776, in *Wealth of Nations*, declared that human beings in a state of nature, when left to pursue their self-interest, are led by an invisible hand (nature itself) to organize society better than anything they could possibly do by design.

To Smith and the Founding Fathers, human beings in society need one thing: a clear set of rules that forbid anyone from depriving anyone else of their natural rights. Beyond that, humans do not need to be told what to do. In fact, our biggest mistake is to organize collectively, wherein we will find ourselves dependent on the ethical behavior and moral restraint of those given power.[17]

The U.S. Constitution is that clear set of rules. No nation has a finer set. No nation has a document that simultaneously creates democracy and then immediately provides a safeguard against its inherent weakness: majority rule—where 51 percent can impose their will upon 49 percent.[18] The Constitution counters that possibility by breaking government into three branches, in which each branch keeps a check and balance on the other two. The process slows down the making of law, but legislative gridlock is a fundamental protection, thus, a fundamental price of freedom.[19]

Democracy, then, is religion: a means, not an end; a process, not a goal. Kept in check by the judiciary, whose sole purpose is to prevent the other branches from passing unconstitutional legislation, the process works as long as the Constitution is taken literally.[20]

As a check on unconstitutional legislation, consider that Chief Justice John Roberts, in his argument supporting the Affordable Care Act [2012], reaffirmed that the commerce clause was not meant to regulate anything other than what the clause's enumerated powers were meant to regulate. Roberts reasoned that if the nation wants universal health care, it was not for the court to say no, but that it *was* for the court to say that the enumerated powers cannot be expanded to justify the Act, that the enumerated powers were not meant to create a national welfare program. The commerce clause, Article 1, Section 8, was not meant to be a problem-solving tool.

Where the Constitution delegates matters to the legislature— taxation, the military, patents—legislators have latitude for interpretation. The court avoided the constitutional issue by calling the Affordable Care Act a tax. That was *not* how President Obama presented the act. President Obama vehemently denied it was a tax. According to legal scholar Timothy Sandefur, the Affordable Care Act is a reminder that this nation lives under a double standard: we protect some rights, by adhering to close scrutiny of the Constitution, but not others, by adhering to what jurisprudence calls "rational basis review." [21]

Rational basis review is the notion that the judiciary must show deference to the elected representatives of the people, that respect for democracy requires that courts uphold legislation if there are rational facts and reasons that could support Congressional judgment, even if the Justices would come to a different conclusion. According to Sandefur, "rational basis" is the progressive inversion of constitutional priorities. In the name of democracy, it is a legal and political elite defining freedom as the right of the collective to enforce its will.[22] To progressives, it is the notion that natural law is complete nonsense. To Oliver Wendell Holmes, law is the subjective preferences of a majority of the people. There are no "transcendental" principles of law because law "does not exist without some definite authority behind it."[23] The idea that the people have certain rights at all times and all places is absurd. Rights are only what a society's power-wielders choose to allow." "All my life I have sneered at the natural rights of man."[24]

Progressives also disrespect the Founding Fathers, whom they see as white, male, class-conscious, parochial skeptics (even about democracy), although they did not sneer at President Franklin Roosevelt's threat to add six justices to the Supreme Court for the purpose of countering Congress' opposition to the New Deal.[25] What President Roosevelt proposed would have ended our system of checks and balances, have ended American democracy.

Yes, rule of the majority *is* a feature of the Constitution, provided the majority doesn't limit freedom without genuine public purpose, and *protection of the minority* is a feature of the Constitution, provided the minority doesn't hide behind "states' rights" to abuse freedom. That's why there is a judiciary: actively to strike down laws, no matter how well-intentioned, that would trample individual freedom.[26]

Even if humans live in a state of nature, they also live in civilized society. We therefore empower government to prevent citizens (whom we know are not all angels) from taking the law into their own hands. But we also empower courts to prevent government from taking the law into *its* own hands. We put a boundary around politics.[27]

2. Public Choice Theory:

Public choice theory (the theory of collective decision-making) reveals that the first priority of a politician and a government bureaucrat, no differently than any person in the private sector, is to look out for his or her own self-interest. That is why, as new public entities are created to solve new public problems, over time, the old entities remain in place. *That* is the explanation for growth in government.[28]

It is also the explanation for growth of special-interest groups.[29] What public choice theory reveals is that when legislatures distribute resources, private interest groups do what they can to obtain it. They will spend on lobbying and suasion up to the point at which their marginal cost equals their marginal benefit—for a military contract, an enormous amount of money. The process: rent-seeking.

Rent-seeking special-interest groups have limited opposition. The taxation that pays for government-distributed wealth is so widely dispersed that individual taxpayers are mostly unaware of what they are paying for and are not, therefore, watching where the money goes. Special-interest groups, fully aware, carefully watch where the money goes—to them. The reality behind public decision-making is that politicians support legislation that provides concentrated benefits to interest groups [who finance politicians] at the expense of unorganized taxpayers.[30]

Yet, when a legislature passes a bill that favors a private party, that is not making law; that is passing judgment. According to Sandefur, it is a command, and not in the public interest.[31] It is politicians working for special interests that abuse the legislative process by purposely creating complex legislation (bundling too many issues into one piece of legislation) to hide their true costs. A voter cannot choose between one candidate and another when hundreds of issues accrete to a candidate.[32] Trading votes, logrolling, makes it possible to pass all legislation brought before Congress, though few of the issues would be accepted if voted on separately.[33]

In light of public choice theory, it's naïve to believe blindly in representative government. Legislatures are agents of the special interests that bankrolled their electoral campaigns. Special-interest groups do not bankroll appointed judges, but the fact remains that unelected judges do make law, and if they are progressive, can be influenced to interpret the law liberally. In *Chevron, U.S.A., Inc. v. Natural Resources Defense Council*, for example, environmental groups persuaded the Supreme Court to reaffirm that government administrative agencies have the power to interpret their legal mandate, in the case of the Environmental Protection Agency, for example, as expansively as it wants, 467 U.S. 837, 844n (1984).[34]

With growth in government the interests of bureaucrats coincide with the interest-groups to which they cater. Government agencies ask for larger budgets to develop information and provide leadership to the groups they serve. "Our administrative state is no longer the quaint model of conscientious legislators deliberating about the public good." It has been placed in the hands of agencies and bureaucrats.[35]

Contrast this with the private sector where the incentive is to produce efficiently, where lower costs translate into higher profits, higher costs into failure. The public sector has no such price index. Price signals are missing from the capital market. According to

Sandefur, when a corporation announces a strategy that committed investors closely personally watching believe to be faulty, the corporation's stock price drops. No such mechanism exists in the public sector and, so, inefficiency is difficult to detect. With no competition to take customers away, bureaucratic leaders pursue their narrow visions without regard for costs relative to benefits.[36]

Bankruptcy weeds out inefficiency in the private sector, but not in the public sector. Failure to achieve a targeted objective, for example, lower crime rates, or higher student test scores, is used as an argument for *increased* public sector funding.[37]

Another problem is that public sector managers seldom gain personally from measures they take to reduce costs. They have no incentive to keep costs down when all they need do is ask for more money—or worse, if they find that they have extra money and that that will cause next year's budget to be lowered, go on an end-of-the-year spending spree.

3. The Constitution:

The Constitution is the instrument by which the people delegate power to the legislature, but when lawmakers go beyond their bounds, citizens must intervene to keep them 'within the limits assigned to their authority by pronouncing their illegal acts unenforceable and void.'

—Alexander Hamilton, *The Federalist Papers 78.*[38]

An analogy: How does a bank (the people) protect itself from the bank guard (the legislature)? With a third party (the judiciary), except that the third party must also be constrained by rules that are not arbitrary (the Constitution), but based on consensual political philosophy (the Declaration of Independence).

In *Clinton v. City of New York*, 524 U.S. (1998) the Supreme Court ruled: The Constitution does not allow Congress to give the President a line-item veto power. The Constitution does not explicitly prohibit the line-item veto, but the Founders wrote down the entire procedure for making a bill into a law. They did not provide any alternative methods; they were 'silent on the subject of unilateral presidential action that either repeals or amends parts of a duly enacted statute' (at 439). The Founders' constitutional silence 'was equivalent to an express prohibition' against Congress delivering any alternative methods of law making. In other words, by specifying one procedure for making and vetoing laws, the Constitution bars Congress from creating others. Congress has no power to give a presidential line-item veto or create any law that contradicts generally understood principles or logical implications of the Constitution.[39]

Even when standards are not fixed, and people disagree on what's implied in the Constitution and the Declaration, in that no law or statement of human design is perfect, people must still try to make work what they agree upon. In America, what was originally agreed upon was the primacy of individual liberty, not the primacy of community. "People in mass are inherently independent of all but moral law," wrote Thomas Jefferson.[40]

Jefferson's statement is normative, about what ought to be but, so, too, are the Constitution and the Declaration—except that the three are based on principle. Positive law, law based on what people actually do, or worse, what they want, populism or progressivism, is law without principle. The Constitution, according to Sandefur, is not a neutral document "made for people of fundamentally differing views, and it is not equally compatible with whatever political or economic perspectives voters or legislatures choose to adopt. The Constitution incorporates a classical liberal political philosophy rooted in individual rights and the promise of lawful, nonarbitrary rule, with courts obligated to enforce these principles even against the majority. Deviating from these standards, adding new constitutional rules or refusing to enforce existing constitutional strictures (that favor the individual rather the community), is wrong. It caters to the worst aspect of democracy—tyranny of the majority."[41]

The Constitution's basic commitment is to the protection of individual rights, not because that commitment facilitates majority decision-making powers, but because individuals need and deserve a shield against democracy.[42] (Democracy is the system we want, according to Winston Churchill, because it is by far the best system we know, but not because it's such a good system.)[43]

This commitment to individual liberty is not what progressives have in mind. To the contrary, progressives seek ways to expand government's powers to overthrow legal precedents they see as obstacles to social programs. This literally is what defines a progressive: belief in collective decision-making. John Dewey, progressivism's leading philosopher, believed that liberty means the individual's effective opportunity to share in the cultural resources of civilization. Dewey believed that lawmakers must create "favorable institutions, legal, political and economic," so as to shape the souls of citizens. "An individual is nothing fixed, given ready-made, but something achieved.[44] And there is B. F. Skinner, progressive's leading psychologist, who believed that moral character is influenced as much by the environment in which one is raised as by one's genetic makeup. It is because of Dewey and Skinner that we have today in the U.S. government social programs that mold the mind and character of the nation.[45]

Progressives believe that inequality of wealth explains immoral behavior—the very reason for government to redistribute wealth and redesign society. Dewey repudiated classical liberal individualism in favor of an organic vision of the good society.[46]

Such is the elitism of progressivism. Its real basis, however, is a progressive's underestimation of the average person. Disguised as "care for the less fortunate," progressives rationalize their willingness to circumvent the Constitution.[47] (Think Napoleon, Che Guevara, and Raskolnikov in Dostoevsky's *Crime and*

Punishment, three individuals who saw themselves as above the law.)

Progressives have been successful because they focused on procedure—on obtaining a desired outcome rather than sticking to immutable principles. Justice Oliver Wendell Holmes agreed. "If my fellow citizens want to go to Hell, I will help them. It's my job."[48]

But there is an immutable principle in the U.S.: individual liberty.[49] Economists James Buchanan, Gordon Tulloch, F.A. Hayek, and Ludwig von Misses consider their work "methodologically individualist," meaning that *everything*, all social, political and economic activity should be explained from the perspective of the individual. This late nineteenth and mid-twentieth-century thought (for which Hayek and Buchanan received the Nobel Prize) is itself the very essence of Western civilization: society should focus on the individual not on its rulers, not on the community; no one has a right to tell others what to do. Western civilization is not a cultural alternative, it is an evolutionary step forward for mankind.

Implied then, is that the solution to most of the world's problems is individual responsibility. The form solutions take will depend on the individual and his or her culture, but individual responsibility cannot be delegated. (Anyone who has ever run a successful business will testify that very often they end up doing everything themselves.) The solution, really, to all the world's problems is "Do It Yourself!"

In *Calculus of Consent*, James Buchanan and Gordon Tulloch emphasize the importance of the fact there are differences among individuals; if individuals were identical, the economy would vanish. There would be no trade. Individuals would all produce the same things, and without surplus. The standard of living would drop to the survival level of the Middle Ages.[50]

The dilemma with respect to methodological individualism, with putting individual liberty at the center of all decisions, is that it is not clear where the dividing line is between collective and individual action. How do we find that dividing line? Buchanan and Tulloch advocate the use of economic reasoning, cost-benefit analysis, to determine the selection of a decision-making rule (which is itself a group decision). How should such rules be chosen —by consensus, democratic majority, elite aristocracy, constitution? From the perspective of methodological individualism, at the constitutional level, *unanimity is* the key. Unanimity is certainly possible for the act of creating democracy, although not for eliminating its inherent problem: majority rule.

Is there a conflict between individual self-interest and concern for the group? According to Buchanan and Tulloch, both the theory of democracy and the market economy are products of the Enlightenment, which did not separate politics and the economy; which recognized that man has many facets, including the spiritual and aesthetic; and which saw nothing inconsistent in the idea that collectively man could lay down a general set of rules and that the rules would respect individual liberty—as long as that decision was unanimous. Collectively, nations would choose democracy (a set of rules) no differently than people in business decide collectively to create a firm: for efficiency. Firms exist for one reason: to get costs down (by doing certain things inhouse rather than jobbing them out). And so too does democracy (let government rather than the private sector do certain things). Cost-benefit analysis shows that with a diverse population, the cost of citizens individually bargaining for every issue is inefficient, that some problems of state are more easily solved collectively. However, when government provides enormous social services, there is an enormous balancing of income redistribution, enormous vote-trading, the political process—all of which are the opposite of efficiency.

What criteria should we use, then, to judge whether the public sector is the right size (not too large or small)? Again, Buchanan and Tulloch give an economic explanation: simple majority voting tends to cause overinvestment in the public sector because it allows the individual to secure benefits from collective action without bearing the full costs. Thinking in terms of government action such that some people are better off while no one is worse off, the Pareto optimal (meaning, "tax the rich"), allows society to rationalize the funding of whatever it wants, which allows voters to incorrectly rationalize that they will gain more than they lose, but does not account for the Pigovian perspective of unseen social costs (municipal and state bonds advertised as, "they will not raise your taxes," yet whose interest payments are added to the city or state's budget deficit).

What if the state does not invest in general welfare, but leaves that to the market? According to Buchanan and Tulloch there would probably be too little investment.[51] Yes, we accept that when government invests, the range of collective activity will expand, yet, according to Buchanan and Tullock, if a society has strong moral or ethical restraints, that need not happen; constitutional curbs on excess will prevail.[52] However, under progressivism, disguised populism, restraint on the allocation of government resources (tax dollars) never prevails.[53]

There may not be correct criteria for balancing government and private provision of public goods, but as long as there is give-and-take in the legislature, as long as everyone remembers that trade is not one-sided, unanimity is still the goal—unanimity and keeping society philosophically based on the individual. Otherwise, the risk of majority rule is *permanent* tyranny of the majority. The New Deal, the Great Society, the transformative statutes of the Warren Court, the Affordable Care Act, none of these will ever be reversed, even though there is large minority and lasting opposition.[54]

Basic Myths about the Market

1. The market is immoral:

Not so. Markets foster consensual trade. In industrialized economies where everyone is dependent on each other, individuals cannot survive if they are dishonest: no one will deal with them. In this self-corrective sense, morality is built into the system. (Citizen consumers are not always informed about what they purchase and so, at times, are taken advantage of, but that's something that will never change.)

2. Markets must be regulated:

No. There is no need for government intervention, for example, to break up monopolies. Monopolies grow naturally from firms buying each other up, except that it's only a matter of time before monopolies become too large and break up as naturally as they were created. Of the 30 firms on the Dow Jones Industrial Average in 1964, three remain today. New technology, change in consumer demand, change in ownership from one generation to the next, firms too big for their own good, all guarantee that monopolies break up.

Then, too, markets have their own regulatory institutions: product rating services, consumer feedback via the Internet, transmission of information via advertising, stock exchanges, and certification boards. Rather than prevent monopolies, paradoxically, government institutes them directly: the U.S. Postal Service, public utilities, public schools. Or, through acts of regulation, creates them indirectly: the 1890 Sherman Antitrust Act to break up railroads (which did the opposite); the 1914 Clayton Act (to try it again); the 1931 Glass-Steagall Act to break up banking (by separating retail and investment banking), which only reduced the number of banks; airline and trucking regulation, which as for railroads, guaranteed rates far in excess of market. Most of these monopolies were deregulated in the 1980s. Airfares, trucking prices, interest rates, all higher than market, all came down.

Today we have Sarbanes-Oxley and Dodd-Frank, two great creators of monopoly. These acts of Congress give an enormous advantage to the nation's largest firms, those with the lowest long-run average costs, because only they can afford to comply—and then use that advantage to buy up their competition. [See endnote *56* below.]

The fact that financial markets are so inherently unstable and financial crises, therefore, so routine, is reason enough to leave markets alone. The main reason for financial instability is that *all* banks are highly leveraged. [A bank that is not cannot compete. See endnote *56*.] Also, banks make long-term loans with money from short-term deposits. When interest rates rise, banks pay their short-term depositors the new rate, yet still collect the old rate on their loans.[55] There is no getting around this—except to prohibit leverage.[56]

3. Creative destruction destroys jobs:

It only appears that way. What is not seen is that automation, outsourcing, and free trade frees labor to work elsewhere. In a vibrant economy, consumers benefit because prices are at their lowest, and the economy benefits because only those jobs that are most needed come into being. In a free and dynamic economy, except during a downturn, there is almost always a labor shortage, one reason the U.S. and Europe look the other way with respect to illegal immigration.[57]

Thus, the notion of protecting jobs from outsourcing is wrong. Firms source inhouse when it's cheaper to handle things within a company, and outsource when it's more expensive. The process is about reducing cost and producing a better product, not about protecting jobs. It's counterintuitive, but job destruction creates more jobs than it eliminates.

4. The market does not provide public goods:

Saying that government must provide public goods because the private sector will not if there is no way to make a profit is not true. There's always a way to make a profit. The classic case is the building of lighthouses: there's no way to charge ships at sea for such a valuable service, especially along a long unpopulated coastline. No, ships are charged when they enter a port.

Can the private sector provide national defense? Of course, it can. If Iraq and Afghanistan can wage war with private warlords, the U.S. can fight back with private contractors. We don't because civilized nations pay their government's military forces to provide national defense.

National defense and services that citizens want furnished by a neutral third party—police and fire protection, court systems—could be provided by the private sector. Government might tax citizens to provide for public education or public health care, but that does not mean that government itself must actually provide those services.

For example, average per-pupil spending for public education in the United States (according to the U.S. Department of Education) is approximately $11,184.[58] For a classroom of 30 students, that's $335,520 a year. $70,000 including benefits is for the teacher, $70,000 to retire school bonds, $20,000 for two administrators, one on-site, one at central office ($100,000 each for every ten classes), $7,500 for a school secretary and custodian ($40,000 secretary, $35,000 custodian, for every ten classes), $22,500 for utilities ($225,000 for water, garbage, gas, electricity, telephone and Internet per ten classes), and $3,500 for repair, maintenance and supplies ($35,000 for paper, books and broken windows for a school of ten classes, an elementary school, for example)). Schools pay no rent or property tax. $335,520 less $193,500 is $142,020 waste. Spending in public education is 40 percent waste.[59]

Forty to 50 percent waste is about right, the norm, perhaps a necessity, for government services. As with the military, waste is a component of any institution operating under the notion that its services must not be calculated only in dollars and cents—because human lives are at stake. This applies to education and health care. Progressives disdain giving citizens their choice between government or private provision. They fear that citizens would opt for the lower-priced market provision, would want to keep the savings differential for themselves—in other words, undo the ideas of progressivism.

Example: union contracts that include health insurance ignore the fact that the cost of health care in the U.S. is three times what it would be in a free market; that if Medicare, Medicaid, and employer write-offs were eliminated, $1,200 a month for a family of four would drop to $400 a month. Saving $800 more a month means $9,600 a year, $288,000 over 30 years ($480,000 over 50 years). That difference is an outright taking. No one ever mentions this; nor that government interference in the market for health care has, in fact, destroyed that market.[60]

Example: The Environmental Protection Agency (EPA) exists because we assume environmental pollution is a market failure. No. Pollution exists because property rights to clean air and water are not enforced. Owners of property adjacent or downstream from a polluting property should be able to sue for their rights to clean air and water. The market solution, the Coasian solution, the least costly solution to negative externalities is that either the polluter pays all affected property owners to leave, buys their property, cleans up the manufacturing, or himself leaves. Without markets, these alternatives cannot be considered: no prices are available for the calculations. Without markets, government intervention reduces everything to a guess.

5. Infrastructure and a legal system are a prerequisite to economic development:

Not true. Infrastructure and a legal system develop *after* an economy has developed. Emerging nations do not need foreign aid until after their economies have emerged. Infrastructure and enforcement of contracts, like cleanup of the environment, like safety standards in building construction, are so expensive they cannot exist without an underlying viable economy. They are not, then, a precondition to economic growth. Foreign aid should go only to those who create wealth, literally to the individual entrepreneur producing a good or service. Foreign aid should never go to the state, to administrators and social workers who haven't any idea how to handle large sums of money, having never earned it themselves; they will be corrupted by powerful leaders.

Markets need contracts to be enforced, but a legal system, like infrastructure, is not a *sine qua non*. Entrepreneurism is. An economy is a supply-side phenomenon in which everything follows from production, from producers, from a culture that produces producers. China has neither infrastructure nor a legal system (that can be counted on), yet its economy is blossoming. Why? Because China's citizens are entrepreneurial. They love money. All the Chinese ask for is a bit of economic freedom.[61]

Africa, Latin America and the Middle East have some economic freedom. Why, then, are so many countries there not economically successful? Culture. That's why it's so unfortunate that Cuba turned communist: Cuba has an entrepreneurial culture. Had Cuba been allowed to keep its capitalist economy, today, Havana, rather than Miami, would be the financial capital of Latin America.

6. Imports eliminate domestic jobs:

Imports are a gift to the people of the nation who receive them at the expense of those nations that produce them. The price differential goes into the pockets of the receiving consumer.

Imports are a blessing for another reason: they force industrialized nations to move from labor-intensive industry to capital-intensive industry, to industry that requires investment in education and technology. Technology, because it leads to higher labor productivity, *is* the source of higher wages. High wages mean that labor is valuable, that the price of all things in terms of labor is low.

The reverse is low labor productivity, labor that is not valuable. Emerging nations have the comparative advantage in producing labor-intensive products precisely because their labor is less valuable. Add entrepreneurialism, however, and it's only a matter of time before their wages and standard of living rise. Like Japan, South Korea, Singapore and Taiwan, China, too, in 30 years, will be importing everything.[62]

7. Markets neglect those who cannot pay:

Shouldn't government provide for those unable to pay for life's necessities—food, clothing, health care, shelter? Don't human needs trump the market?

What about the fact that a market economy provides a higher standard of living than any other economy, that markets have no problem providing food, clothing, health care and shelter? Why would a nation want a socialist economy? Why would a nation want to nationalize charity (or subsidize business), and then deal with nationwide rent-seeking, with everyone trying to grab some of that public assistance?

Why would a nation nationalize education and health care? Are citizens so afraid of markets that they would rather overpay than allow provision by the private sector? Do citizens believe that government funding means government provision?[63]

8. Economic problems can be resolved through the political process:

How can there even be a political process when the Left believes a nation's economy (and resolution of its economic problems) must have a governmental component, and the Right believes a nation's economy should be left alone (that markets have their own self-corrective mechanisms)? Does political compromise mean that government steps in sometimes, but not

83

always, or steps in only halfway? Does political compromise mean that citizens abandon some principles, but not others?[64]

Does compromise mean the U.S. Constitution should no longer limit government solely to the protection of life, liberty and property, but rather allow it to provide for the nation's welfare *and* accommodate change in public opinion, progressivism," for example, which demands that government apply the latest theories in education, psychology and the social sciences to lead the nation forward?[65]

Why did President Obama agree with the latter? Because he is not a man of principle. During both his presidential campaigns he firmly said that he had no patience with ideologues, that he was a pragmatist interested in breaking through gridlock to solve societal problems, that he was not interested in changing the system. The Affordable Care Act was his crowning achievement. No president before had been able to make universal health care a law. In common with Franklin Delano Roosevelt (who threatened to completely dismantle the Constitution's separation of powers by adding six justices to the Supreme Court for the purpose of passing unopposed any legislation he desired, the Social Security Act, for example) and Lyndon Johnson (who expanded social services simultaneously with the war in Vietnam to bring the nation's budget deficit to a level beyond which we will *never* escape), so, too, Barak Obama, with the Affordable Care Act, has enabled the U.S. to cross a major hurdle on our march toward European socialism.

Yes, President Obama proved that great political compromise is possible. No longer will the nation have to deal with the market for health care; that market is gone. No longer will 45 million citizens be without healthcare. Those citizens have been socialized.

Is any of this important? To people successful in business, none of this is important. Government intervention, an obstacle to go around, is always factored into price. These Confucian philosophers know that unless government intervention comes unannounced, for example, a central bank suddenly and

84

dramatically raising interest rates, that "rational expectations" and "Ricardian equivalence" predict that as soon as they sense government regulation on the horizon, consumers and persons in business will immediately adjust their actions.

In 1970, at age 24, I was a student working my way through college at an expensive woman's shoe store and noted that when President Richard Nixon announced his intention to combat inflation (besides taking the U.S. off the gold standard) by launching wage and price controls, immediately, literally the day of the announcement, the price of every pair of shoes in stock jumped 20 percent.

Basic laws of business, economics and government reveal a key to political compromise: make Congress provide thorough cost-benefit analyses for proposed legislation. If Congress can't decide (because their hands are tied by special interests), let citizens decide. Let citizens choose whether to eliminate government intervention in the market if they believe that the price of the goods and services would drop in half. Why wouldn't citizens want to pay less for health care and education? With lower prices, why wouldn't government be delighted that very few people would then need assistance?[66]

————

Finale

This book makes two points:

1. Career earnings and wealth are two separate matters. Anyone earning minimum wage, by giving a little thought to how money works, can acquire assets and become financially independent.[67]

2. Social, political and freedom are inherently
   interconnected. The degree to which a society
   restrains one of those freedoms is the degree to
   which it restrains the other two.[68]

Point number one implies that citizens can choose a career irrespective of its income. Be an artist; open a restaurant. You may not make much money; it's not important. What's important is that during your career you acquire some assets. In the end, for Café Flor no differently than for Boise Cascade, profit is in the real estate: the underlying real estate rises in value and the mortgage pays off.[69]

Point number two implies that if a nation desires freedom, it must accept the risks that come with freedom. The greatest risk is that citizens lose their nerve and replace freedom with equality. Only socialism ensures equality. With socialism, however, citizens lose the incentive to excel, literally, the force that drives an economy, and also lose an understanding about to what extent all things are relative, that there is no such thing as intrinsic or objective value, no such thing as equality. Without a corresponding loss of social, political and economic freedom, there is, then, no such thing as security.[70]

The loss of incentive to excel explains the dilemma of underdevelopment. If material wealth is not a cultural priority, then neither will be the protection of private property, nor the creation of economic institutions. Societies that reject material wealth also reject advanced health care, institutions of higher learning, high standards in building construction and environmental protection. Very expensive, these cannot be paid for without wealth. There are many ways for individuals to live their lives, but there are only a few ways to live prosperously.[71]

Poor nonindustrialized societies obtain their gains only from trading simple production. They never realize the large gains possible from trading specialized production—or the gains from capital-intensive production, the most profitable.

86

But to industrialize, a state must protect private property. *That's all.* If citizens have a desire to produce, everything else— economic development, rule of law, democracy—will emerge naturally. The state can encourage development, but it cannot make it happen—not even under communism. The idea that economists, under the guise of science, as engineers, can create the ideal society is a vision from another era.

India still lives that vision. India's government is an active player; it provides money, except that rent-seekers siphon off most of the profit, which in turn is not reinvested. China learned (the hard way) not to do that. China puts a straw in the milkshake, slurps a cut of the action, but because it wants the economy to grow, leaves it alone. Two forms of corruption, except China will flourish; India will stagnate.[72] India still thinks it can direct the economy: determine aggregate levels of consumption, investment, public spending, full output, full employment. All from an era where economists thought they knew the precise manner in which the multiplier effect worked, that an increase in government spending would translate into an increase in aggregate demand, output and employment (not to mention social well-being). That was an era when economists thought that they could acquire information about daily life and plan effective policies.

Economists know better today. They know they do not have that information: either economists are students, and the state is a referee of the economic game, or economists are saviors, and the state is an active player.[73]

Control of an economy, socialism, even if it resolved problems of production and consumer demand, would not create entrepreneurialism, the force that both generates and coordinates an economy. To determine value, entrepreneurialism is dependent upon price signals which do not exist in a socialized economy. Economic knowledge of the change in billions of bits of information for billions of people every second of the day—what price signals reveal—is not something planners can grasp. Only individuals actively engaged in a particular activity at a moment in time are able to use those signals, and even then, are only able to pull out information that is relevant to them. Otherwise, economic information is completely beyond computational accessibility.

Still, the most profound reason not to control the economy is that an economy, like humanity, like all organisms, is a product of nature. It does not need help. At moments of natural catastrophe (or for individual citizens, major personal crises), yes, government might step in, except that at those moments people normally help each other—including people who wouldn't otherwise.

I worked in a real estate office where the conversation, in 1972, was horribly racist. One day an older black man walked in the front door and said, "I'm very thirsty. Can I have a glass of water?" The most racially offensive of all those present literally dropped what he was doing, ran to the rear of the office and brought the man a glass of water. "Are you all right? Is there anything I can do for you?"

In 1989, after the Loma Prieta earthquake in San Francisco, with all traffic signals down, drivers were extremely courteous to each other: cars that arrived first, passed first. Traffic flowed on its own. Everyone thought, "Why can't society be like this all the time?"

Because that's not how life works. We instinctively cooperate during a natural catastrophe or when we see someone suffering personal distress. Otherwise, morality is a function of self-interest. We behave well to others because we want others to behave well to us—because we are dependent upon one another. Unless you are self-sufficient and have no need to sell your products or your labor, a reputation for fraud is a death sentence. See Adam Smith, 1759, *The Theory of Moral Sentiments*.

Do we need government? Do citizens of a nation need to be controlled? Control is censorship. We don't censor speech. The ACLU goes out of its way to defend the KKK's right to speak in public precisely because once a nation picks and chooses who it will defend, it immediately loses what legs it has to stand on to prevent censorship of the political ideas that *it* prefers. This nation was founded on the Jeffersonian notion that everyone be allowed to vote, that nations afraid to let the common man vote have nothing. But that also applies to the economy. Nations afraid to let citizens trade among themselves without government interference have nothing. The nondynamism of socialism is the road straight to serfdom.

According to populist historian A. J. P. Taylor, back in 1914, "a sensible law-abiding Englishman could pass through life and hardly notice the existence of the state, beyond the post office and the policeman. He could live where he liked and as he liked... Broadly speaking, the state acted only to help those who could not help themselves. It left the adult citizen alone."[74]

AFTERWORD

New York Times columnist David Brooks asserts that in the world of political economy, a writer sits somewhere on the spectrum between engaged and detached. Engaged is a writer who seeks to mobilize people to action, for example, through their political parties. Detached is a writer who seeks to teach, to reveal underlying realities.

Personally, I am detached, but for a different reason: as a person successful in business I am indifferent to political ideology. As a "Keynesian animal," I am aware of politics (and may use them to my advantage), yet I am also aware that politics perverts, that business transactions mixed with politics contain the seeds of a nation's destruction—by encouraging transactions that do not stand on their own merit, for example, based solely on tax benefits, and by encouraging government participation in the economy, which only leads to national debt. That is why our Constitution established government as a neutral third party: to protect life, liberty and property; *and*, to protect the nation from its own government, from growth in government, which inexorably comes at the expense of individual freedom. The Founders understood, as do those in business, that government intervention confuses citizens about a basic truth of living in a free nation, namely, that citizens are responsible for their actions.

APPENDIX A

Gay Talese

...My father had left Italy two years before Benito Mussolini had brought the country under his fascist control, and while my father had been outwardly pro-American throughout World War II, I never recall having heard him say anything in the privacy of our home that was condemning of Mussolini. My father believed that the Italians required a strong leader, being disorganized and undisciplined as a people. He often quoted to me Mussolini's line: "Governing the Italian people is not impossible, merely useless."

I think my father left Italy with great misgivings about his homeland, disappointed with its low status as a world power, lower than that of the French, barely higher than that of the Greeks, its government in Rome unstable and inefficient and unable to adequately feed and shelter its people, and having no social conscience—driving people like himself, among the most ambitious and restless members of his generation, out of the country forever. Despite all his piety and sense of obligation to those dearest to him, my father was, in my imagined way of thinking, an inwardly angry and very selfish man when he left home, and I further believe that when he came to live in America, he blended his anger and self-centeredness into the melting pot of a nation motivated by millions of men like himself, dissatisfied and driven, coming originally from Europe, Asia, the Middle East, South America, wherever—a diverse group of newcomers who had in common a quarrel with where they had come from and who, unlike many of their relatives who remained behind, had the gall and gumption to say good-bye.

—Gay Talese, *A Writer's Life*, New York, Random House (2006), pp. 169-171.

APPENDIX B

Two McDonald's Employees: San Francisco, California 2019

$15.59	per hour—minimum wage in San Francisco (January 2019)
x 8	hours a day
$124.72	

$23.38	per hour overtime (time-and-a-half)
x 2	hours a day
$46.76	

$171.48	a day
x 6	days a week
$1,028.88	

$1,028.88	a week
x 52	weeks a year (including two weeks paid vacation)
$53,501.76	

$53,501.76   a year
      x 2   people
$107,003.52

Less:

$8,025.25   Social Security tax, 7.5 %
 8,025.25   Federal tax, 7.5%
 2,140.07   State tax, 2%
$18,190.57

$107,003.52   Gross income
 - 18,190.57   Total tax
$88,812.95   Net income
 - 28,800.00   Savings per year (32.4% of net income)
$60,012.95   Net spendable per year

The cost of living in San Francisco:

Rent on a large one-bedroom apartment in San Francisco is $3,000 a month, yet, if shared with another couple, is $1,500 a month.

If the couple live in one of the condominiums they buy, their living expenses will be lower:

[The $450,000 condominium would have a mortgage of $363,600 with interest at 4% per annum amortized over 30 years. The down payment would be $86,400, with each owner contributing $28,800. The three owners expect rent from the condominium, $36,000 ($3,000 a month x 12), to cover their expenses plus generate a 1% cash flow of $4,500 a year.]

Income:

    $36,000 $3,000 a month rent x 12 = yearly rent

Expenses:

5,275	Property taxes per year in San Francisco, with add-ons, are approximately 1.17% per annum
2,400	Property insurance
1,655	Water ($50 monthly), garbage ($35 monthly), gas and electricity (50 monthly), telephone ($35 monthly)
2,880	Repair, 8% of yearly rent
2,880	Capital improvements, 8% of yearly rent
$15,090	Total expenses, 42% of yearly income

Net income:

    $20,945   Income less expenses

Mortgage:

    $18,829   Annual mortgage payment.

Cash Flow:

    $2,116   Net income less mortgage. ($616 more than expected.)

Rent:

    $18,000   Annual rent of $36,000 divided by two (because Asset No. 1 is shared with another couple)

$1,500   Monthly rent

Tax deductions:

Interest payment on the mortgage, $3,078 (4% of $230,880 divided by three), is subtracted from the couple's gross employment income.

In year two, there will be a depreciation deduction from gross employment income of $4,016 each year, and for *each* $150,000 investment they subsequently acquire.

[The deduction is 3.57% of their share of the value of the building, $112,500 (which is 75% of the value of the property, $150,000), for a period of 28 years (100% total depreciation divided over 28 years = 3.57% per annum), which is $4,016 ($112,500 × 3.57%).]

Cash flow from each investment is added back. For each property, cash flow of $2,116 is subtracted from depreciation of $4,016. Starting in year two, and continuing each year thereafter, for tax purposes, the couple's gross income will be reduced by $1,900 ($4,016 - $2,116).

Total tax deduction:

$3,078   Mortgage interest

  4,016   Depreciation

- 2,116   Cash flow
$4,994

Their gross income of $107,003 drops by $4,994 to $102,009.

98

7.5% federal income tax calculated now on $102,009 decreases from $8,025 to $7,650; and 2% state income tax decreases from $2,140 to $2,040. The tax savings is $475 per year [($8,025 - $7,643) at 7.5% plus ($2140 - $2,040) at 2%], $39 per month.

Monthly rent in year two:

$1,500	
- 256	Mortgage interest ($3,078 divided by 12)
- 39	Federal and state tax savings ($475 divided by 12)
- 158	Depreciation minus cash flow ($1,900 divided by 12)
1,047	Adjusted monthly rent

Living expenses:

When agencies such as the Bureau of Labor Statistics determine cost, living expenses are often figured as: housing (30%), food and groceries (15%), transportation (10%), utilities (6%), health care (7%), and miscellaneous expenses such as clothing, services (including repairs) and entertainment (32%). Taxes and savings are not included.

The question, however: living in an expensive city such as San Francisco, during the first few years of their investment program—before the deductions kick in—can the couple survive on $60,012 a year (the original net income of $88,812 less $28,800 savings)? Housing alone, at 30% of that net income, will be $26,643.

Housing	(30%)	$26,643
Food and groceries	(15%)	13,321
Transportation	(10%)	8,881
Utilities	(6%)	5,328
Health care	(7%)	6,216
Miscellaneous	(32%)	28,808
Total	(100%)	$60,099

The couple has no money to spare.

However, they have ways to increase their net spendable:

- Some utilities and housing repairs are already calculated in the housing expense, plus, three tax deductions lowered their rent from $1,500 to $1,047 a month.

- As employees of McDonald's, they receive two meals a day.

- As employees of McDonald's, their health insurance is provided.

- Transportation: walk to work.

- McDonald's provides a 401(k) pension plan. The amount of an employee's contribution reduces gross income for tax purposes, but is taxed when withdrawn for investment. Still, some employers will match the employee contribution, meaning the couple would have more to withdraw.

- Tax deductions increase every year.

- They attend McDonald's University and become more highly paid employees.

Yes, the couple can work at McDonald's at minimum wage, save $28,800 a year, and live on $60,012 a year, but if they move to Sacramento, California, where rents are lower, the example is more realistic.

Is this whole scenario unrealistic? No. It is the scenario for immigrant families in the U.S.

APPENDIX C

Capitalism

Today's socialism, European socialism, is an economic system in which citizens voluntarily give half their income and some amount of ownership of the means of production to the state. The desire for socialism, the universal desire to help those less fortunate, is why so many free-market industrialists, Andrew Carnegie, John D. Rockefeller and today Bill Gates and Warren Buffet give away their fortunes. Even the great free-market economist Milton Friedman said, "If socialism means helping the less fortunate, I'm a socialist."[1]

Still, such philanthropy is possible only in a rich nation. Only a rich nation has the luxury of paying the state, a third party, to provide healthcare, childcare, education, services that citizens normally provide for themselves. Poor nations cannot afford the inefficiency.[2]

Karl Marx understood this. In "The Accumulation of Capital," Part VII of *Das Kapital*, Marx explains that nations cannot distribute wealth before they earn it, although afterward, as an inevitable act of historical materialism, they will. To Marx, socialism emerges from capitalism. He thought Germany, Britain or the United States, not Russia or China, would embrace socialism. But it wasn't until 1932 that a rich nation, Sweden, finally gave it a try, a good try, because, in spite of all the shortages it experienced, Sweden kept at it for 44 years.[3, 4]

———————

Capitalism is a much better idea: apart from low taxes, citizens don't contribute to the state. The state does nothing for citizens, markets provide goods and services, and as a function of the price system, resources are distributed efficiently. If they have entrepreneurs, capitalist nations produce the highest standard of living possible.[5]

An oversimplification? No. Simplification is the essence of science. It is how we make sense of a complicated universe: understanding life as formulae. Simplification, abstraction, use of models, the Laffer Curve, those in business use them to survive. At personal financial risk, tethered to reality, business people have no time for utopia.[6]

The Laffer Curve

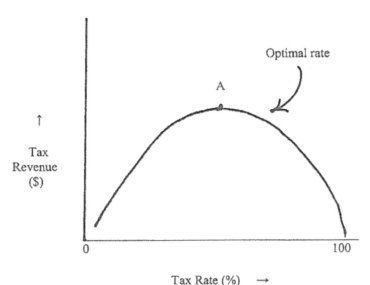

The Laffer Curve shows that low income tax rates do not impede a rise in the nation's tax revenue: they do not impede earned income. However, as tax rates approach point A, the curve flattens, because the increased tax rate caused the *rate of increase* of earned income to drop to zero. Beyond A, the rate of increase turns negative (because of a loss of incentive to produce), and as the tax rate approaches 100 percent, both tax revenue and actual earned income drop to $0. The Laffer Curve reveals that once the tax rate passes point A, the state receives ever less revenue.[7]

What those in business know is that can you can't tax the poor: they have no money; you can't tax the rich: they won't pay; you can only tax the middle class: they don't know how not to pay. It's unfair because tax on the middle class is in relative dollars, a large percentage of their wealth, whereas tax on the rich is in absolute dollars, a small percentage of their wealth. This suggests the correct solution: low or no income taxes. That will encourage the rich to earn and invest more (put people to work), and to repatriate their money.[8, 9] The Laffer Curve, a model from supply-side economics, is correct: Don't tax Atlas!

APPENDIX D

Entrepreneurial Mindset

All economists love the following quote:

The ideas of economists and political philosophers, both when they are right and when they are wrong, are more powerful than is commonly understood. Indeed the world is ruled by little else. Practical men, who believe themselves to be quite exempt from any intellectual influences, are usually the slaves of some defunct economist. Madmen in authority, who hear voices in the air, are distilling their frenzy from some academic scribbler of a few years back…There are not many who are influenced by new theories after they are twenty-five or thirty years of age, so that the ideas which civil servants and politicians and even agitators apply to current events are not likely to be the newest.[1]

Written by John Maynard Keynes, one of the world's most famous economists, this expresses what all economists believe, namely, that they, especially in relation to people in business, have the bigger picture.

Keynes was an economist, not an entrepreneur. What Keynes and most economists do not fully appreciate is the extent to which the thought process of an entrepreneur (or lack of one) is so completely different from that of an economist. For one, the entrepreneur is indifferent to economics—and politics. He or she is also indifferent to the technical problems of a transaction, to the existence of government regulation, even the current financial situation. All of this is secondary to a gambler's instinct. When operating in the dynamic, at the moment, the ideas of economists and philosophers are irrelevant—why Keynes, an intellectual, is as famous for having said "practical" men operate simply on "animal instincts."[2]

Those animal instincts, however, *are* the entrepreneurial mindset—the ability to use intuition (timing), judge character (poker), and ignore risk (shoot from the hip).

Analysis comes later. Getting control of an asset—getting it under contract, putting up a deposit—that comes first. Only then are you in a position to discover the true facts. Then, perform your analysis.

Such entrepreneurial hardiness (audacity, bravery, hence the word foolhardiness), requires training, no differently than any genuine skill—sports, art, teaching—that requires knowing what to do without having to think.[3] Knowing when to stop what you are doing, to walk away, even after a purchase, that also takes practice. If you can't play from "you win some, you lose some," you're not an entrepreneur. If you're not willing to drop money from time to time, you're not an entrepreneur.

Does analysis even play a part? How is it possible, with any certainty, to determine net present value (discounted cash flow analysis) when it's not possible to accurately determine future cash flow, when future gross revenue less expenses are a guess? What is the appropriate capitalization rate?

And when are investors ever presented with more than one investment at a given time? Even professional investors are lucky ·to be presented with one viable investment. In the market, in the real world, deals are made, not found. Comparison is not a primary consideration.

Consider dyslexia. Dyslexics are drawn to running their own businesses, often several at a time. Why? Because their inability to read efficiently is compensated precisely by what is necessary for success in business: good judgment and the ability to delegate *every* aspect of management. As reported by Brent Bowers, "Tracing Business Acumen to Dyslexia," *The New York Times*, 12/6/07, a study from the Cass Business School in London found that 35 percent of entrepreneurs (and only one percent of corporate managers) were dyslexic. They excel in oral communication and creative problem solving precisely because they learned how in childhood to compensate for a handicap. Childhood strategies for survival, including the ability to grasp the big picture, and persistence, provide the perfect training for entrepreneurs to stay away from paper, to focus instead on people, on intuition. The founders of Virgin Galactic, Cisco, IKEA, Jet Blue, Kinkos, Charles Schwab, Turner Broadcasting, Ford, and Hewlett-Packard were dyslexic.

The following elements of negotiation are part of the entrepreneurial mindset and reveal why a dyslexic, for that matter anyone with a third-grade education has an advantage over the overly educated. When operating in the dynamic, consider the following:

1. Panic. Howard Hughes certainly did not panic. On the contrary, his policy was: do nothing (which makes sense for a recluse). Knowing that no one likes to wait—agents counting their commission, sellers counting their profit, buyers anxious to show what they've purchased—Hughes knew that one of these three would crack, would take the initiative, would do something, but by doing something, change everything—in his favor.[4]

2. Timing. There is a beginning, middle, and end to every transaction. If you don't panic, if you can wait until the last minute to sign documents, the

eleventh hour, you will be in a position to improve the deal. With buyers, sellers, and agents impatient to close, someone will concede something they shouldn't. Not quite honest [and not practiced by me], it *is* the thought process of an entrepreneur, one that calculates that at-the-very-last-moment is where the deal is—that negotiation up to that point was diversionary.

3. Deals are possible in any market. When the market is down, you push price even lower by paying all cash. When the market is up, you compensate for high price with terms. You negotiate to pay the high price 15 years from now, when the asset may be worth it: you purchase with a promissory note. If the payments are high (because price is high), you structure them as an overall rate of return. If interest is six percent, you pay three percent years one through five, six percent years six through ten, nine percent years 11 through 15 (with a right-of-first-refusal to purchase the note should the holder decide to sell it later at a discount).

4. Value-added. Still, price and terms are secondary to a genuine vision as to how to add value to an asset. Richard Branson started Virgin Airlines at a time when there were more than enough airlines, all of which were struggling, and against the advice of those on his board at Virgin Atlantic. The vision: focus on the customer and provide great service and entertainment. That doesn't seem like a vision, but if the competition is not doing it, it is. Was Branson shooting from the hip? According to Branson there is an art to risk taking, to knowing which chances are worth taking and which are not. Branson simply leased one old Boeing 747 for a year to see if it

would work. It did, so, in year two he leased a second plane.[5]

The above are examples of entrepreneurial thinking, not formulae. They reflect a mindset that never says, "It can't be done," a mindset that intuitively grasps the underlying truth of a transaction—the true demand for a product, the true nature of an asset,[6] a mindset that does not understand the meaning of the word, "no." [The French love the word, "no" [*non*], but that's also because they have no word for "entrepreneur."]

For an example of a nonentrepreneurial mindset, consider the conclusion drawn by the author of *The Economist* article, "Corporate Saving in Asia, a $2.3 Trillion Problem," cited in "Timeless Rates of Return," endnote *11*, Chapter 2, footnote **. The author mentions that Japanese and South Koreans are sitting on trillions of dollars in savings, yet spending none of it. To that author, that is the Keynesian "paradox of thrift."

> If East Asia's firms spent even half of their huge cash hoards, they could boost global GDP by some two percent.

Voilà, the liberal solution: solve problems by spending money. Obviously, the author has never produced a product, never experienced fear from working from too low a cash base, never grasped the fact that entrepreneurs, one percent of the world's population, are *the* central component in a market economy and that if they're not confident, the economy comes to a halt. It's not for an economist to tell an entrepreneur to borrow money and start production simply because the population has high savings (or because millions of people are unemployed).

Like economists, so, too, are government employees an example of a non-entrepreneurial mindset. Rather than address the real problem in public expenditure, diminishing marginal utility of the funds, government simply asks for more funds. In education, for example, funding doubled between 1970 and 2000, yet, in inverse relation, test scores dropped.[7] Why do educators still ask for more money, still complain that their failure is due to a lack of funds, when any business person presented with these facts would propose the very opposite: cut funding to raise test scores?

Cuba is an example of a nonentrepreneurial mindset. Cuba represents the socialist-communist mindset that finds entrepreneurs so distasteful they are literally chased out of the country. Ditto, in France.[8] The problem, however, is that socialist redistribution rather than capitalist creation of wealth causes an economy to come to a halt. In Cuba, the latest model automobile is a 1959 Chevrolet.

Tragic, also, because socialist redistribution of land is an impossibility. *Farm workers are not farmers.* Farming is a skill requiring investment in machinery, a college degree in agriculture and knowledge of world commodity markets. Farming requires knowing what crops to plant and how to plant. It requires a profit incentive to spur technological innovation and efficient production —precisely why China abandoned communism in agriculture, gave that industry back to the people. ["Sorry, folks, that was a mistake!"]

Plus, socialist-communist economies have no replacement funds for old machinery and infrastructure. Why? Because oil, gold, loans or confiscated wealth do not sustain an economy. A nation's natural resource is its people.

The following example from my own business dealings demonstrates the entrepreneurial mindset:

In 1993, at the height of the 1990s S&L scandal, interest rates were high, and the economy was in recession. A real estate agent sent me a letter advertising 22 units for sale. I responded. The agent said it would be a difficult purchase, that the seller was a tough negotiator, and that he, the agent, had sent the flier simply as a way to maintain contact with his buyers. I replied: "Deals are made, not found. Arrange a meeting with the seller."

At the meeting there were three brokers, the seller and me. I instructed the brokers not to say a thing, that I would do all the talking. I said to the seller, "Sir, the market is down, interest rates are high, and banks are not lending. So, I'll pay you your asking price; I'll use my contacts to obtain a loan; and you will carry back the balance of the purchase price with a promissory note." The seller agreed. Surprised that he agreed, I then said, "There is one more condition. From your proceeds, I want you to lend me an additional $60,000 (in 2019, $240,000 in the San Francisco Bay Area)." The seller agreed. The leveraged buyout developed, thus, into a cash-to-buyer transaction. I did not allow the agents to talk precisely because agents are not entrepreneurs, precisely because they would never have allowed me to make such an offer.

APPENDIX E

Margaret Thatcher

As she prepared to make her first leadership speech to the Conservative Party conference in 1975, a speechwriter tried to amp up her enthusiasm by quoting Abraham Lincoln:

> You cannot strengthen the weak by weakening the strong.
> You cannot bring about prosperity by discouraging thrift.
> You cannot help the wage-earner by pulling down the wage-payer.

When he had finished, Mrs. Thatcher fished into her handbag to extract a piece of ageing newsprint with the same lines on it. "It goes wherever I go," she told him.[1]

According to *The Economist*, the quote is a fair summation of her thinking, that societies must encourage and reward risk-takers, entrepreneurs who *alone* [my italic] create the wealth without which governments cannot do anything, let alone help the less fortunate.[2]

Margaret Thatcher believed that profligacy and borrowing are the road to perdition, that socialism and communism are evil, and that a strong state and free economy are essential to prevent such ideas. In Britain, as the only political leader ever to be able to break the power of labor unions, to force the Labor party to abandon its commitment to the nationalization of industry, she earned the title "Iron Lady."

Thatcherism is the second theme of this book, that economic freedom and individual liberty are interdependent. So certain of this, and oblivious to life on the street and the exigencies of *realpolitik*, she stated:

> I am not a consensus politician; I am a conviction politician. I came to office with one deliberate intent, to change Britain from a dependent to a self-reliant society, from a give-it-to-me to a do-it-yourself nation."[3]

After her early victories, however, that overly blind pursuit was her undoing. The Labor Party (any labor party!), always the embodiment of populist mediocrity, lacking in principle yet high in emotion, made a comeback. That is probably man's destiny. Thomas Jefferson unhappily admitted 250 years ago that "the natural progress of things is for liberty to yield, and government to gain ground."[4]

APPENDIX F

Karl Marx 1859

A Contribution to the Critique of Political Economy[1]

PREFACE

The reason to include this Preface is to let you experience the language and thought process of Karl Marx. So foreign and dense, it should put everyone on guard. There is no forerunner to such thought: the language and ideas are medieval scholasticism—not the free ideas of Western culture.

To advocate for a completely new and untried economic system for the world, for hundreds of millions of people, without any idea of how it would work, what the social, political and economic consequences would be, in history, there is no precedent. How could the whole world have taken Karl Marx so literally?

Hegel. Marx and Friedrich Engels jumped on Hegel's notion that every thousand years or so there is a complete change in how the world understands things. *That* was their basis for advocating whatever came to their mind. Consider the following excerpts from the Preface [with my comments in brackets]:

> In the social production of their existence, men inevitably enter into definite relations, which are independent of their will, namely relations of production appropriate to a

117

given stage in the development of their material forces of production. The totality of these relations of production constitutes the economic structure of society, the real foundation, on which arises a legal and political superstructure and to which correspond definite forms of social consciousness. The mode of production of material life contains the general process of social, political and intellectual life. [Actually true: the reason for a free economy.]

It is not the consciousness of men that determines their existence, but their social existence that determines their consciousness. [For a better world, just change social existence—with violence if necessary.]

In studying such transformations it is always necessary to distinguish between the material transformation of the economic conditions of production, which can be determined with the precision of natural science [the essence of progressivism], and the legal, political, religious artistic or philosophic—in short, ideological forms in which men become conscious of their conflict and fight it out. ["All political power grows out of the barrel of a gun."—Mao Tse Tung.] Just as one does not judge an individual by what he thinks about himself, so one cannot judge such a period of transformation by its consciousness, but on the contrary, this consciousness must be explained from the contradictions of material life, from the conflict existing between the social forces of production and the relations of production. [Change relations now, ask questions later.]

No social order is ever destroyed before all the production forces for which it is sufficient have been developed, and newer superior relations of production never replace older ones before the material conditions for their existence have matured within the framework of the old society. [Society cannot leap from agriculture to

118

communism. Capitalism is the middle step, the framework of the old society.]

The clearest arguments to counter socialism were written immediately after the first printing of *The Communist Manifesto* (1848) by Frédéric Bastiat, in *The Law* (1850), in which socialist fallacies were exposed to their unseen consequences. The book has been in print every year since. Its explanations and arguments are still used—the principal argument being that *every* economic action has an unseen consequence, and that upon examination, unseen consequences reveal that socialist arguments lead to a lowering of the standard of living.

Hegel was right. Every thousand years or so, society does make a change—in which, in the case of communism, emotion replaces reason, and everyone knows, in their heart, that they are right.

APPENDIX G

Arrow's Paradox

Traditional democratic theory depends on majority voting. Agreed is that a majority of some group of people will decide the issue. Several economists in the past, Condorcet, for example [late 1700s], wondered if a majority always really represented the genuine will of the majority, wondered to what extent *paradox* [this author's italic] might be a part, i.e., that in fact, because of intricacies of the voting process, that a majority vote did not in the end represent the majority will.

That happens when a majority is forced into existence as the result of restricting choices, for example, by eliminating candidates over several rounds of voting... where all possible alternatives can be voted on in a series of pairs, each against each of the others, and the one which beats all of the others can reasonably be considered to have majority support. The paradox is that the winning candidate does not represent the genuine will of the majority.

—James M. Buchanan and Gordon Tullock, *The Calculus of Consent* (cited earlier), pp. 328-330.

Mitt Romney represented the Republican Party in the 2012 U.S. presidential election. He beat various Republican candidates in the primary elections in various states, yet he did not represent the genuine will of the majority of the Republican Party. Voters nationwide sensed that. Had the Republican Party fielded a candidate as strong as Barak Obama, the Republican candidate would have won. Barak Obama, like Jimmy Carter, would have lost to a Ronald Reagan.

Pitting alternatives against each other in pairs (as primaries often do) may not lead to a satisfactory result, because a genuine majority occurs only cyclically, not constantly. According to Kenneth Arrow, who received a Nobel Prize for his proof, there is no voting rule that will lead to "the will of the majority."

Voter 1	Voter 2	Voter 3
A	C	B
B	A	C
C	B	A

With these three voters and these three candidates (A, B, C), these are the possible combinations:

Voter 1 prefers candidate A to B, B to C;
Voter 2 prefers candidate C to A, A to B;
Voter 3 prefers candidate B to C, C to A.

B beats C for two out of three voters, and A beats B for two out of three voters. A, therefore, should beat C, except that for two out of three voters, C beats A. Thus, reality in a democracy is that if majority rule is cyclical, the will of the majority will prevail two out of three times.

If two out three voters genuinely prefer A, there is no problem: A wins, but that is usually not the case. Democracy requires compromise, voting trading, logrolling—which in the end creates a majority, but not a genuine majority. If there are only two candidates in a series of elections, the winner will probably represent the majority, but as more candidates enter the race, the possibility increases that the winning candidate will not.

In large elections, where an individual's particular vote does not make a difference, where the candidate who wins is not necessarily the one who represents the majority, the implication of the opening statement, page one, of this entire book is corroborated:

> For an individual, the most fundamental of all economic goals is financial independence—freedom from worrying about the state of the economy, from following the news every day, from producing a product and making a profit. [Now add, "from needing to vote."]

Another reality of voting is that in political elections, most people focus on the candidate, not on the issues. The exit polls for the 2012 presidential election showed, for example, that on the major issues, Americans agreed with Mitt Romney, that they didn't like Obama's record on jobs, the economy, or "Obamacare," but when it came to the key question—which candidate cares more about people like me?—Romney was blown away, 81 percent to 18 percent.[1]

As per the voter's paradox (a result of the cyclical presidential primary process), Mitt Romney did not represent the will of the majority, but he lost also because the reality of elections is that the skill at which each party portrays their candidate rather than his or her ideas trumps everything, including the need for the two parties even to debate each other.

APPENDIX H

Thomas Piketty

Capital in the Twenty-first Century[1]

Sentence one:

> The distribution of wealth is one of today's widely discussed and controversial issues.

[The issue is irrelevant. Bill Gates has a lot of money, and the world is far, far better off having given it to him. His company, Microsoft, produced a product, a computer operating system, that makes everyone's life more efficient—both at home and at work. Henry Ford did the same. Has Mark Zuckerberg done the same? We'll know in 50 years, but the question, then and now, is still irrelevant.]

Sentence two:

> But what do we really know about wealth evolution over the long term?

[In a free and industrialized economy, wealth distribution varies according to 60-year business cycles; its evenness rises and falls as a function of the creative destruction of industry and wealth. Of the 30 companies on the Dow Jones Industrial Average in 1964, three are there today.]

Sentence three:

Do the dynamics of private capital accumulation inevitably lead to the concentration of wealth in ever fewer hands, as Karl Marx believed in the 19th century?

[Piketty says, "No." He's right! But superficially, because capital accumulation does lead to a great body of wealth in a small percentage of the population—for a good reason: see "Sentence Thirty" below.]

Sentence four:

Or do the balancing forces of growth, competition and technical progress lead in later stages of development to reduced inequality and greater harmony among the classes, as Simon Kuznets thought in the 20th century?

[Piketty says, "No." He's wrong! Of the 74 Nobel Prizes in economics since 1969, 55 have been awarded to American economists, 28 from the University of Chicago, almost all for their proof of market efficiency. Piketty still believes the rich have become wealthier at the expense of the poor, that basic forces in a capitalist economy are the cause, and that the inequalities of capitalism undermine democracy. Piketty advocates a global "wealth tax."[2] That is pure zero-sum thinking—reasoning that one person's wealth must be at the expense of another. That's not how economists reason.]

Sentence eleven:

There are nevertheless ways democracy can regain control over capitalism and ensure that the general interest takes precedence over private interest...

[Should we toss out the economic lessons of the last 250 years which show that an economy, like life itself, is organized by an invisible hand, in which everything living pursues its natural interests, that it is not possible for the general interest to gain

126

control over capitalism (which is also the goal of fascism and communism)? Should we toss out everything we have learned from *Wealth of Nations*?]

Sentence thirty:

There is no escaping the fact, however, that social science research on the distribution of wealth was for a long time based on a relatively limited set of firmly established facts together with a wide variety of purely theoretical speculation.

[Irrelevant. There is no need to analyze an economy. Most wealth is earned as a function of production. Secondly, in free-market supply-side economies, great wealth is always concentrated in the top one percent of the population: they're the ones with the drive to obtain it—more importantly, the ones that drive the economy, its *sine qua non*.]

Page two:

The distribution of wealth is too important an issue to be left to economists, sociologists, historians and philosophers. It is of interest to everyone, and that is a good thing.

[Populism. Wealth and democracy spring from economic opportunity—think Machiavelli. Distribution of wealth, relative, even absolute, is not the issue. Production and economic growth, *that* is the issue.]

Page six:

The price system plays a key role in coordinating the activities of millions of individuals—indeed, today, billions of individuals in the new global economy. The problem is that the price system knows neither limits nor morality.

[Creative destruction in nature and the economy has nothing to do with morality. Not knowing that markets self-correct, that governments can do nothing to regulate an economic cycle, *that* is the problem, *that* is what leads to socialism—fascism from the right, communism from the left, in the twentieth century, 120 million dead.]

Page twelve:

…What is more, before the requirement to declare one's income to the tax authorities was enacted in law, people were often unaware of the amount of their own income. The same is true of the corporate tax and wealth tax. Taxation is not only a way of requiring all citizens to contribute to the financing of public expenditures and projects and to distribute the tax burden as fairly as possible; it is also useful for establishing classifications and promoting knowledge as well as democratic transparency.

[Data in the hands of central planners to put into practice their socialist ideal of forcing the rich to pay high taxes (which, thanks to advances in data collection "we" might finally know what they own and how much they earn), is what *Capital in the Twenty-First Century* is all about—except that this nonlibertarian belief runs counter to everything "we" have learned from Adam Smith, that individuals pursuing their natural interests organize society better than anything that can ever be planned by design. Piketty, writing as if he were not an economist, thinks that his readership, not educated in economics, will not question his utopian vision, a 0.5 percent world wealth tax, and his cherry-picked data to show that wealth inequality is approaching apocalypse.[3]]

Page twenty:

What are the major conclusions to which these novel historical sources [of data collection] have led me? The first is that one should be wary of any economic

128

determinism in regard to inequalities of wealth and income.

[A complete rebuttal to classical economic theory.]

The history of the distribution of wealth has always been deeply political and it cannot be reduced to purely economic mechanisms.

[A complete rebuttal to the driving forces behind the United States of America freedom and opportunity, the chance to make it on one's own, *the* dream of every immigrant. (Note, Piketty is French, and what he says may be true for France and elsewhere in the world—ask any French entrepreneur, most of whom live in London—but it is not true for the U.S.—a self-selected population all of whom came here precisely to flee that concept, that nonentrepreneurial mindset.]

The second conclusion, which is at the heart of this book, is that the dynamics of wealth distribution reveal powerful mechanisms pushing alternately toward convergence and divergence [of equality]. Furthermore, there is no natural spontaneous process to prevent destabilization in egalitarian forces from prevailing permanently.

[A complete rebuttal to Adam Smith's *Wealth of Nations*. Paying lip service to the economist Simon Kuznets (to whom he refers frequently), Piketty admits that inequality does drop at the beginning of industrialization, as in China today, yet adds that afterward, it rises permanently.]

Page twenty-five:

This fundamental inequality, which I will write as $r > g$ (where r stands for the average annual rate of return on capital, including profits, dividends, interest, rents, and other income from capital, expressed as a percentage of its total value, and g stands for the rate of growth of the economy, that is, the annual increase in income or output), will play a crucial role in this book. In a sense, it sums up the overall logic of my conclusions [that inequality widens as the rate of growth of capital exceeds the rate of growth of the economy].

[See "Timeless Rates of Return," Chapter II of this book, in which it is stated that the timeless rate of return on savings is one to two percent, mortgage lending two to three percent, and venture capital four to five percent. If the growth rate of an economy is approximately the growth rate of its population, in the U.S. three percent per annum, then the growth rate of capital, i.e., its timeless rate of return, does not exceed the growth rate of the economy. If the population isn't growing, possibly neither is the economy—in which case growth occurs only if productivity rises (the creation of goods or services with ever less capital or labor)—nor returns on capital.[4] Piketty's solution to *his* notion that the growth rate of capital is greater than the growth rate of the economy is progressive taxation: those with high income are to give most of it back such that $r = g$. See Chapter 15 below.]

Page thirty-three:

...Income, capital, the economic growth rate and the rate of return on capital are abstract concepts—theoretical constructs rather than mathematical certainties.

[*Capital in the Twenty-First Century*, or this book, *Income and Wealth*; one of these belongs in the garbage.]

Chapter 15, "A Global Tax on Capital":

The primary purpose of the capital tax [wealth tax] is not to finance the social state, but to regulate capitalism. The goal is first to stop the indefinite increase of inequality of wealth, and second to improve effective regulation on the financial and banking system in order to avoid crises. To achieve these two ends, the capital tax must first promote democratic and financial transparency: there would be clarity about who owns what assets around the world.

[Piketty received his doctorate at age 22 and immediately became a professor of economics. His lifework, then, is based on a student's first political awakenings. Had he not been so smart so young he would have matured before writing *Capital in the Twenty-First Century* and included some discussion of how, exactly, society will confiscate wealth from the rich. It's not enough to simply state that a nation's government will announce as of a certain date that the rich will start paying an annual 0.5 percent wealth tax. Are the rich just going to hand it over? (If your assets exceed $10 million, hand over $50,000 a year in addition to your income tax even if you do not have the money, such as most property poor farmers, and despite the fact that the money will *not* be used for social services but simply to reduce nationwide inequality by reducing the value of your personal assets.) As they do for all other taxes, won't the rich just pass the tax cost along as a price increase on the goods and services they produce?

Plus, in a constitutional democracy that protects a citizen's right to privacy, where does the state obtain the right to know exactly what you own? And how would the state obtain such information? Again, no discussion, except that Piketty says the state would no longer have to rely on "the archaic method of asking all persons to declare honestly how much they own" (page 521), that this information would be obtained, like property taxes, by an automated data system linked to your tax return and updated annually. Information on bank balances would also be transmitted automatically—as well as on all banks in the Cayman Islands and Switzerland. Big Brother, good luck!]

> Obviously this [wealth tax] has nothing whatsoever to do with the principles of the market economy. No one has the right to set his own tax rates. It is not right for individuals to grow wealthy from free trade and economic integration only to rake off the profits at the

expense of their neighbors. This is outright theft. (Page 521.)

The benefit to democracy [wealth tax] would be considerable: it is very difficult to have a rational debate about the great challenges facing the world today—the future of the social state, the cost of the transition to new sources of energy, state-building in the developing world, and so on—because the global distribution of wealth remains so opaque.

[Again, a complete rebuttal to classical economics—which explain that wealth is a function of production, not distribution, inheritance, or the ownership of the means of production; that markets will always provide new forms of energy if consumers are willing to pay for it; and that pollution is controlled by enforcing property rights to clean air and water, not by regulating industry. In dynamic economies most wealth is earned; in nondynamic economies, lost—think aristocracy in Europe. Think *The Wealth of Nations*, not *Das Kapital*, not *Capital in the Twenty-First Century*.]

APPENDIX I

Atlas Shrugged

> I swear by my life and my love of it that I will never live
> for the sake of another man, nor ask another man to live
> for mine.[1]

The above quote, pure Ayn Rand, pretty harsh, is still better than, "From each according to his ability to each according to his need," pure Karl Marx, pure rubbish, pure refutation of John Adams' "We are a nation of laws, not men," the understanding in law that justice precedes mercy—that we don't break the law because we feel sorry for someone such as a single unemployed mother of three children being evicted from her home with nowhere to go, and require that the landlady, a single unemployed widow who were it not for that rent, would herself be thrown into the street, come to her aid.[2]

To take from one person to give to another: that's socialism. In the West, the community does not take from the individual. Individuals have the right to their life, liberty and property, natural rights protected by law that, by extension, protects achievement and pursuit of self-interest, *the* foundation of economic growth, *the* reason why the West is prosperous.[3]

This is the message of John Mandeville in *The Fable of the Bees*, of Adam Smith in *The Wealth of Nations* and *Theory of*

Moral Sentiments, in the twentieth century, of Ludwig von Mises in *Human Action, a Treatise on Economics*, F. A. Hayek in *The Road to Serfdom* and Ayn Rand in *Atlas Shrugged*.

The message is that you do not ask for the product of someone above you because you need it. That gives someone below you the right to the product of your ability. In a dynamic industrialized society, economic equality is not a concern; it is in constant flux. It is personal achievement that counts.

> ...every form of happiness is one; every desire is driven by the same motor–by our love for a single value, for the highest potentiality of our own existence—and every achievement is an expression of it.[4]

Replace competition to produce a product by competition to show greatest need, and the economy will collapse, as did in 1989 the Soviet Union.[5]

Atlas Shrugged is about an economy grinding to a halt because the nation (U.S.) turned its back on objective truth, on who it is that holds up the world, Atlas, a nation's producers.[6]

Fortunately, the U.S. is not the Soviet Union, although the New Deal, Great Society, rulings of the Warren Court, and legislation such as the Affordable Care Act push it in that direction. U.S. business has not yet withdrawn its services, moved as in *Atlas Shrugged* to an artist colony to wait out the fall of an intolerable political-economic system, but, in the Soviet Union, it did withdraw. As in her novel, business did live under a "Directive," similar to conditions in George Orwell's *1984* and *Animal Farm*, and Aldous Huxley's *Brave New World*, to resurface, unfortunately, as unscrupulous oligarchies.

In the U.S. today, that "brave new world" is the politicized public schools. At age 24, at the commencement of my teaching career, coincident with the appearance of multiculturalism (the idea that Western civilization is just one approach), I understood that the career before me would be in the service of a system in decline.[7] I could have withdrawn and chosen not to serve; instead,

I followed through and paid the price. At times badly treated, as a libertarian among progressives, I thought I could work independently. Like the industrialists in *Atlas Shrugged*, my mistake, then, was to work within the system. Like those industrialists, I, too, did not recognize that the integrity of my own work would be used against me; for example, while I was made to feel unwelcome, my successful concerts were used to showcase how well my schools "appeared" to be doing.

By the end of my career the hypocrisy had completely backfired. On the day of my spring concert (at an elementary school where I had a huge instrumental and choral program), just before going on stage, the principal approached me and said, "I can see that you have more children on stage than in the audience, that your curriculum is truly multicultural, that the level of performance at this school has never been higher, but don't come back next year; you don't belong; you're not one of us."

A year later, I took students from one school to another to create a combined orchestra. The understanding was that on the day of the performance how many students would be allowed to go —fifth-graders first, then fourth, then third—would depend upon how many parent drivers showed up (not simply volunteered). I told the only third grader that she would probably not go, but promised to take her next year. Sure enough, we were short a driver. And sure enough, her Latina mother complained to the Latina principal, who, then, said, "Watch this!" and made a phone call to central office. After 15 years at that school but only one for the new principal, she had this Caucasian author transferred to another school. Why she couldn't drive the student herself or give the mother and daughter bus fare to travel ten blocks is not clear. What is clear is that mother, child and principal were "entitled."

The final straw was the state of California's latest "Directive": All Teachers Must Enroll in A Two-Year Course In Multicultural Awareness. After 40 years of intensive multicultural teacher training at great public expense, education bureaucrats at the state capital, anxious to show that they had something new to

135

offer (i.e., save their jobs), decided that Euro-centrism and teacher insensitivity to the cultural needs of minorities was the problem, that California teachers, ranked among the nation's best, with masters' degrees in education from the University of California and Stanford, were to blame for the drop in ranking of California's public schools from first in the nation in the 1960s to near last from the year 2000 on.

I asked for an exemption. I indicated that I understood the problems of nonnative speakers, having been a foreign student myself, that I had a foreign language teaching credential, spoke four languages and was genuinely appreciative of all cultures, having performed professionally with musicians of all ethnic backgrounds as well as having taught inner-city public schools for 40 years. Denied the exemption, I was told, "If we do this for you, others will ask for it (plus we know older teachers like you will refuse, and we can replace them with younger teachers at half the salary)."

In my last year I showed up for work in September, following detailed instructions as to where to report for the first days of teacher meetings. After several hours I noticed my name was not on the sign-in roster. Someone suggested, "You'd better run down to Human Resources and resign—immediately. You are about to lose your health insurance and maybe your pension." My gamble, that the District would not really enforce its absurd directive, didn't pay off.[8]

Perhaps what didn't pay off was 40 years of political incorrectness, for example, returning from summer break and making remarks such as, "Where is Ms. Jones, the school's best teacher? And, "Where's Suzy, my best trumpet player? Did they move to an artist colony?" Not appreciated. Both had withdrawn their attendance. Suzy transferred to a private school; Ms. Jones quit. For the last 30 years, according to the California Commission on Teacher Credentialing, 50 percent of new (meaning young, bright, enthusiastic, well-trained) teachers left within three years; 75 percent within five years. The statistic speaks for itself. The less obvious statistic is that over a 30-year period, when one teacher per year and one student per year leave, no one is left—except those at the bottom; no mystery, then, that California test scores are at the bottom.[9]

How did that happen? One reason is that California, conforming to a nationwide vogue, forces teachers to "teach to the test," the most unZen, unWaldorf, unprofessional approach possible. This *diktat* only serves to push out the most creative students and teachers, even administrators, to satisfy that vague "community" need for equality of outcome (rather than individual achievement). Couple it with equality of input, paying the worst teachers the same as the best, giving the worst students the same attention as the best, and *voilà*, you have a major reason for the scholastic results of political correctness.

Transfer that politicized formula to private industry and you have the story of *Atlas Shrugged*, in which the private sector is rewarded [subsidized with state assistance] for failure rather than ability, in which objective standards of excellence are replaced with relative standards, in which the rights of industries in need take precedence.

The solution for the public schools is the solution and principal action in *Atlas Shrugged*: an *owner's* strike. "Workers of the world, *you* try running an industry!" "Parents of the world, *you* try teaching in a public school!"

Socialists assume that society can change just one thing, ownership of the means of production, or ownership of the schools, and that nothing else will change: that the industrialists whose property you confiscated will stick around to help operate their former factories, that teachers well prepared to teach British and American history, culture, and democracy will stick around to coach their multicultural replacements.

For a reality check, consider these passages from *Atlas Shrugged*:

> We've heard it shouted that the industrialist is a parasite,
> that his workers support him, create his wealth, make his

luxury possible—and what would happen to him if we walked out?

I propose to show to the world who depends on whom, who supports whom, who is the source of wealth, who makes whose livelihood possible and what happens to whom when who walks out.[10]

What do they think is the driving faculty of those who discover how to use oil, how to run a mine, how to build an electric motor? That sacred fire which is said to burn within musicians and poets—what do they suppose moves an industrialist to defy the whole world for the sake of his new metal, as the inventors of the airplane, the builders of railroads, [today, computers, tomorrow, space travel], the discoverers of new germs or new continents have done through the ages? ...An intransigent devotion to the pursuit of [objective] truth.[11]

For if there is a more tragic fool than the businessman who doesn't know that he's an exponent of man's highest creative spirit—it's the artist who thinks that the businessman is his enemy.[12]

A principal insight from *Atlas Shrugged*:

I had accepted the one tenet by which they destroy a man before he's started, the killer-tenet: the breach between his mind and body. I had accepted it, like most of their victims, not knowing it, not knowing even that the issue existed. I rebelled against their creed of human [social] importance and I took pride in my ability to think, to act, to work for the satisfaction of my desires. But I did not know that this was virtue, I never identified it as a moral value, as the highest of moral values, to be defended above one's life," because it's that which makes life possible. And I accepted punishment for it, punishment for virtue at the hands of an arrogant evil, *made arrogant*

138

solely by my ignorance and my submission [emphasis added].[13]

With one finger, I tapped two students on the wrist to get them to stop talking. The parents of these students asked for a full hearing before the principal to resolve the incident. Their dysfunctional home life caused them to continually act up to get attention, yet, those two students would never miss my class. I allowed them to remain for the very reason that for my entire teaching career I taught their age level, namely, that when I was their age, ten, I was them.

Running scared, the principal said to me, "I will script the entire meeting; tell you exactly what to say. The last thing I want is the Board of Education coming here to question me about following their directives."

APPENDIX J

1984: George Orwell

The Party seeks power entirely for its own sake. We are not interested in the good of others; we are interested solely in power, pure power.

We are different from all the oligarchies of the past in that we know what we are doing. All the others, even those who resembled ourselves, were cowards and hypocrites. The German Nazis and the Russian Communists came very close to us in their methods, but they never had the courage to recognize their own motives. They pretended, perhaps they even believed, that they had seized power unwillingly and for a limited time, and that just around the corner there lay a paradise where human beings would be free and equal.

We are not like that. We know that no one ever seizes power with the intention of relinquishing it. Power is not a means; it is an end. One does not establish a dictatorship in order to safeguard a revolution; one makes the revolution in order to establish the dictatorship. The object of persecution is persecution. The object of torture is torture. The object of power is power.[1]

[Tongue in cheek? No. Power comes by frightening a nation into submission. (According to Chairman Mao, "All political power grows out of the barrel of a gun.")

Leaders of the Party, however, are still human. That is what Winston Smith repeated (until he succumbed to torture): that it's not possible to control a population through "doublethink" (where words mean their opposite—but not always) and perversion of reality (rewriting history to eliminate unwanted facts) without some people knowing the truth. That is what caused the Soviet Union to collapse: not only leaders but everyone realized that everything was a lie.]

NOTES

Chapter One

1. In 1949, with the arrival of television, he sold the theaters.

2. Professional investment may require cash, with the understanding that the cash will be recaptured by subsequent financing. In real estate development, if cash is used to purchase the land, it is recaptured within the ensuing construction financing. In venture capital, cash is put up front, followed by years of waiting (while the product is developed), but in exchange, and also because of risk, return on investment is far in excess of other investments (although when averaged with the nine out of ten venture capital investments that fail, return may not be any higher). [For capital structuring purposes, some assets are held free of financing, for their cash flow, while others are fully leveraged for their tax write-offs. For diversity, capital is sometimes held as stored wealth, as art, land, or precious metal.]

For example, I took inspiration from my grandfather's solution. Confronted with an enormous negative cash flow from overpaying for a 40-unit apartment building just before the market crash of 1990 (the S&L Crisis) I solved that problem by selling the building at a loss, yet immediately purchased three other properties from owners in the same position, i.e., who had also overpaid. I used 100 percent leverage, *plus* demanded that the sellers each loan me $60,000 in cash [$240,000 in 2020], adding to the leveraged buyout the element (frowned upon in the real estate business) of "cash-to-buyer."

3. See Appendix A for a realistic account of who immigrates to America.

4. The uncontrolled freedom of American culture and capitalism is blamed for the extinction of the native populations of both people and animals. That, however, is modern analysis. Eighteenth and nineteenth century immigrants from Europe, reeling from centuries of persecution by privileged aristocracy, and pillage from constant warfare, were upon arrival in North America, as settlers moving west, again subjected to danger—the danger and isolation of living in wilderness. Surrounded, literally, by two million wolves, their farms on the prairie trampled by 200 million buffalo, then picked off one at a time by Indians, that was their reality. See "The Story of American Hunting and Firearms," *Outdoor Life Magazine,* New York (1976), Sunrise Books/E.P. Dutton & Co., Chapter 5, "The Battle with the Wolves," p. 53 and Chapter 9, "The Slaughter of the Buffalo," p. 95. They did what they had to: eliminated the wolves, the buffalo and the Indians (no differently than Rome, after much warfare and fear of the Carthaginians, eliminated Carthage (3rd Punic War); no differently than the West, if Islamist terrorism becomes intolerable, may eliminate the Middle East once and for all). Yes, greed was part of it, but greed is part of human nature, exists everywhere, and does not always lead to bad things. It spurred migration west, the Gold Rush of 1849, and spurs business in general. The pursuit of profit has led business to do more to alleviate poverty, foster creativity and promote understanding across cultures than any other institution. History's worst examples of greed, precisely because not accounted for or worse, denied, were communist Soviet Union and China—whose very *raison d'être* was to eliminate greed by creating equality of wealth and guaranteeing basic human services. Yet, wherever they exist, communist governments expropriate all land and possessions and redistribute them as they see fit, in theory to the proletariat, in reality to themselves, members of the Communist Party. [When the proletariat press for their share, they,

144

too, are eliminated—60 million in China and Russia (see Appendix J, *1984*).]

Greed cannot be eliminated, but exploitation, its close cousin, can be: privatize all land and resources, and then enforce property rights so that owners of land adjacent to owners who pollute or destroy natural resources are able to force resolution. Native Americans were crushed precisely because they did not have property law. Fish in the sea are overfished precisely because they have no property rights in the sea: tragedy of the commons.

In the U.S., greed may have spurred westward expansion, but actually settling that land led to the realization that it was in everyone's self-interest to cooperate. Unruh makes the statement that it was not only rugged individualism but enormous collective cooperation that made this nation what it is. Cooperation existed with the first overland migrations in the East before the American Revolution, and again with overland migrations west before the Civil War. About this point, Unruh concurs with noted American historian Daniel Boorstin, *America before the Revolution and the Civil War*.

5. Andrew Carnegie, *The Empire of Business* (1902), New York, Books for Business, 2001.

6. Carnegie continually reaffirmed his belief in education and in lifelong study, but understood that business is not learned in school; that if you study business in college, you will not want to start at the bottom which means that you will never rise to the top. If you have never worked in the mail room or swept the lobby, you do not know what you did not learn. The policy at McDonald's is that *all* chief executives start at the bottom. See *The Economist*, "Fries with That?," 4/27/13.

7. It's easier to start with high income, but like nations with vast natural resources, starting with income and resources is usually a curse: it dulls the drive to succeed. Except for the U.S., none of the richest nations in the world have natural resources— Japan, Britain, Netherlands, Singapore, Hong Kong, Taiwan and South Korea.

Having zero wealth to start with slows the process, but only at the beginning. The blessing in disguise is that individuals are forced to focus on what it is they are doing, because only then will they be able to convince others to finance their endeavors.

8. The national average in the fast food industry is $9.24. McDonald's Corporation pays on average $9.40 an hour (January 30, 2019, *PayScale.com*).

9. "Poverty: The Decathlon of Deprivation," *The Economist*, 3/23/13, p. 79.

By UN standards, Americans do not live in poverty—which is why entitlements should be eliminated. Eliminate Medicare, Medicaid, and employer write-offs for health insurance, which together create a higher than market demand, thus higher than market price for health care. Eliminate low deductibles for health insurance so that consumers pay some of the bill themselves; as a consequence, themselves force health care providers to stop charging so much and performing so many unnecessary procedures —in other words, change health insurance so that it is no longer pre-paid health care but simply insurance, and the price of health insurance will drop 66 percent, to about $400 a month for a family of four. (See David Parker, *Healthcare*, Chapter 1, www.davidparkeressays.com.) Eliminate Social Security so that individuals create their own pension accounts with future payouts not dependent upon people working in the present, as now, in the U.S., where half as many work as are retired, and those retired depend upon the unsustainable government-promised return of eight percent, rather than the real market return of four percent.

By any measure, Americans do not live in poverty. Americans living on Indian reservations, in Appalachia or in the rural South, do so by choice. As Europeans judge the Roma, we judge those peoples—from our materialistic perspective. *Their* perspective is that, "If we wanted to work, we would; we would work at McDonald's."

And McDonald's is always looking for employees, especially employees who want to move up. Those employees are sent to McDonald's University. There's one in London, for example. Lured there by Margaret Thatcher when she was a Member of Parliament, it is one of the largest training centers in all of Europe. See *The Economist*, 4/27/13, p. 60 (which also mentioned that McDonald's was rated by the *Sunday Times* as one of the best 25 employers in England). [This writer brought his music students, after their Spring Concert, to a particular McDonald's in San Francisco. Surprised that after four years the manger was still the same person, he asked why it was that she was still there. Her response: "You can't tell from the outside, but this McDonald's is the largest in Northern California. I'm well paid." If the above *The Economist* article is correct, that some McDonald's franchises in England take in £5 million a year, then, that particular San Francisco McDonald's may very well be taking in $10 million a year.]

Chapter Two

1. The starting point for any science is the world as we find it, as perceived through the senses. From there, through trial and error, we induce and deduce the laws of nature—and by extension, human nature. We do this also as a check on natural human behavior, even if we do not all agree on what natural human behavior is. We do this as a check on human ideas, one of the worst being that government should intervene in the economy. The French, for example, believe that intervention in an unbridled economy is absolutely a fundamental mark of civilization. Yet, it is the complexity of human behavior—enormous cultural and individual differences—that is the key to the conscious organization of human society: don't do it! No animal species consciously organizes itself. No animal species has leaders that "tell" others what to do. John Gray, in *Straw Dogs*, puts it this way:

> Darwin showed that humans are like other animals,
> humanists claim that they are not. Humanists insist that

by using our knowledge we can control our environment and flourish as never before. In affirming this, they renew one of Christianity's most dubious promises—that salvation is open to all. The humanist belief in progress is only a secular version of this Christian faith.

In the world shown us by Darwin, there is nothing that can be called progress. To anyone reared on humanist hopes this is intolerable. As a result, Darwin's teaching has been stood on its head, and Christianity's cardinal error—that humans are different from all other animals— has been given a new lease on life.

> —John Gray, "Science versus Humanism," *Straw Dogs:* Thoughts on Humans and Other Animals, 2002, New York, Farrar, Straus and Giroux, p. 4.

Gray further states:

The idea of humanity taking charge of its destiny makes sense only if we ascribe consciousness and purpose to the species; but Darwin's discovery was that species are only currents in the drift of genes. The idea that humanity can shape its future assumes that it is exempt from this truth. *Ibid*, "The Mirage of Conscious Evolution," pp. 5-6.

Bernard Mandeville in *The Fable of the Bees* (1732) had this insight. Mandeville's example was a colony of bees in which all activity supports the hive, "as if" it were communally self-directed. Adam Smith placed that insight at the center of *Theory of Moral Sentiments* (1759) and of *Wealth of Nations* (1776), with the conclusion that society is always organized, naturally, "as if" by an invisible hand. It is why John Locke could state that the sole purpose of government is simply to protect this natural state, to protect individuals' natural right to their own life, liberty and property. The very essence of Western civilization, then, is that the individual should be the focus of society, that the rights of the individual precede those of the state.

A modern approach to societal organization is James Q. Wilson's *The Moral Sense* (1993). "Order exists because a system of beliefs and sentiments held by members of a society sets limits to what those members can do." Cited by David Brooks in "Rediscovery of Character," *New York Times*, Op-Ed, 3/5/12, Brooks explains that order will exist in any society as long as a majority has the same beliefs and, according to Wilson, if society reinforces quality of character—essentially individual responsibility. To Brooks, Marxists look at material forces, Darwinians at competition, public policy makers Right and Left think about the arrangement of economic incentives, but Wilson reduced it to quality of character.

What Wilson should have said is that like natural behavior in bees, morality, and quality of character are encoded in our genes. Although they can be weakened in childhood, morality, and quality of character are essential to our survival as a species (in that those who kill are themselves eventually killed, ensuring that the psychotic gene is eliminated—almost).

2. In "Steel, an Inferno of Unprofitability," (July 6, 2013, p. 57), *The Economist*, reports that the world's overcapacity in steelmaking is getting worse, that profits are evaporating. According to the article, the importance of an industry does not necessarily translate into financial success, that, in fact, steelmaking scrapes by on microscopic margins [why governments everywhere subsidize their steel mills]. Still, it was oversupply and overcapacity, the natural result of overexpansion of credit, a weakness in human nature, that caused the 2008 financial crisis— merely the latest in the long history of man-made crises. In 2012, in Europe, oversupply and overcapacity led to a contraction in demand for steel, according to *The Economist*, to 145 million tons, 30 percent below its pre-crisis level. Europeans with their high labor costs had pushed the price of steel too high. Deals struck when times were good (as with real estate in the U.S.) came back to haunt.

3. In April 2001, John Hammergren took over the McKesson Corporation, a wholesale supplier of drugs and health-care supplies. At the time, McKesson's stock price was $27 a share. Today [July 2013] it is $115 a share. According to *The Economist*, July 6, 2013, p. 58, that rise is about 325 percent—in a period in which the S&P index rose 40 percent. Hammergren's combined rewards (pension, options) over the period represent about three percent of the $19 billion increase in the company's stock market value, about $570 million.

4. From the perspective of acquiring personal wealth quickly, wealth is a function of acquiring assets through the use of leverage. However, in terms of the timeless rates of return on capital, in the long term, wealth is a function of capital expansion—the creation of surplus production of real goods and services. [Surplus production is the Marxian definition of capital.] The true definition of wealth, even the Marxian definition, is that wealth is always a function of production. See Adam Smith, *Wealth of Nations*, 1776.

5. Workers cannot protect themselves from the cost of taxation and regulation being passed back to them as lower wages and higher consumer prices. They cannot protect themselves by taking over the means of production and returning profit to themselves. Profit doesn't exist.

People in business know how to exploit taxation and regulation, to use loopholes, but people in labor do not. To compensate, labor unions, whose actions are enforced by government, legally raise the price of labor above market. That in turn raises the overall return on capital projects, including government projects, precisely why the Mafia loves labor unions: there is so much money to be skimmed.

The drive to obtain an above-market return is natural human behavior: it caused the 2008 financial crisis. It pushed banks to become finance companies—lenders that borrow from outside sources rather than from their own depositors, and in the process lose their natural inclination to be cautious. Banks loaned to anyone by instructing borrowers, on their loan applications, to lie about their income. Banks wanted only one thing: commissions and loan fees. Not interested in a normal return, the spread between the interest they pay depositors and what they charge borrowers, they wanted the above-market return of a subprime mortgage. Banks turned away from traditional personal relationships with people they knew toward one-time transactional relationships with people they did not know (and didn't care to know). They acted in ignorance of the timeless rates of return and of the probability of an economic downturn as a result of their over-expansion of credit. Considering the damage, why aren't those bankers in prison? Because our government decided there were too many banks too-big-to-fail (TBTF), and that there were too many people to imprison (TMTI). What if Mayor Giuliani, who cleaned up crime in New York City, had thought there were just too many people? That was not his answer. Giuliani said, "Drop a candy wrapper on the sidewalk, go to prison." Everyone got the message.

With any severe punishment there is injustice that will affect some individuals, but this is compensated by its public usefulness.

—Tacitus, *Annales XIV* (55-120 AD),
cited in *The Essays* of Montaigne

[In other words, what counts is the surety of punishment, not the severity.]

Even more fundamental, the 2008 financial crisis was caused by government. Starting with President Bill Clinton, with his policy of "anyone in America who works full-time and has good credit should be able to own a home," banks were pressured to make subprime loans. Government agencies, Fannie Mae and Freddie Mac, were pressured to buy those loans—knowing they were fraudulent—to immediately resupply the banks with money to make more loans.

That is a far cry from the classical liberal notion upon which this nation was founded: that the sole purpose of government is to protect life, liberty and property—not intervene in the economy.

Since the 1930s, we have been walking away from that notion. This is why the city of Richmond, California [2014] considered eminent domain as a way of getting property owners off the hook of continuing to pay on mortgages that were too high. With eminent domain, the city of Richmond wanted private investors to buy those mortgages at fifty cents on the dollar and sell them back to the original property owners for sixty cents on the dollar (with monthly mortgage payments at 60 percent). Unfortunately, there is a moral issue here. Pension funds that bought bonds secured by those mortgages, that provide retirees a lifetime return, would, instead of being protected by government, be wiped out by government. Allow eminent domain for this purpose, and every lender in the country will stop lending—or compensate by doubling the interest rate they charge on any new loan they make. The whole nation will be made to pay for those Richmond homeowners who, having lied on their loan applications, now, won't accept responsibility for the purchase or refinance of the $250,000 home that is today worth $125,000, won't wait a few years for price to come back—don't even realize how lucky they are, in the San Francisco Bay Area, to have a home with only a $200,000 mortgage.

The counter-argument is: why should government bail out sophisticated banks, crooks, but not first-time home buyers? Why does business take the moral high ground when *it* is owed money, but when it *owes* money, expects to be bailed out?

Another counter-argument is that since people in business make money off everything that government does (which is why they contribute equally to both political parties), nothing that government does should be considered immoral. (Still, a distinction should be made between an immoral action countered by an amoral action and an immoral action countered by an immoral action—government authorization of subprime loans followed by business compliance versus business fraud.)

6. Health care in the U.S. is a problem because its price is three times what it should be. Government intervention in the market for health care—Medicare, Medicaid, tax write-offs for business, the illegality of purchasing health insurance across state lines—pushes demand three times higher than what it naturally would be (plus eliminates the incentive for consumers themselves to monitor price). With health insurance for a family of four $800 a month ($9,600 a year) higher than it should be, our nation's standard of living has been compromised.

7. John A. Allison, in *The Financial Crisis and the Free Market Cure*, 2013, McGraw Hill, New York, pp. 18-19, states why government intervention is not the cure to a nation's economic problems:

> ...because human beings are not omniscient, markets are constantly correcting. Poorly run business, or businesses for which customer's demand has changed, go out of business, and new businesses that do a better job of meeting consumer demand are created. A free market is in constant correction. It is always searching for the best way to produce goods and services at the lowest cost and the best quality.
>
> When the Federal Reserve steps in and uses monetary policy [such as Quantitative Easing I, II and III] to stop the downside correction process, all it achieves is to defer problems to the future and make them worse. Its action delays and distorts the natural market correction process, thereby reducing the long-term productivity of the economic system by encouraging a misuse of capital and labor. One of the best ways to view free markets is as a great number of experiments that are being conducted simultaneously. Most of the experiments are failures. However, every failure contributes to the learning process. Thomas Edison noted that the 1,000 apparently failed experiments that led to the light bulb were, in fact, absolutely necessary. For every Google or Microsoft there are 1,000 failures, all of which are in a certain sense necessary.

8. How can war possibly be good for an economy? The civilian unemployment of eight million before World War II was simply exchanged for eight million military jobs—with 405,000 killed and 670,000 maimed. (Wikipedia). The average workweek increased 20 percent—with some employees, engineers, working 14-hour days, seven days a week. National output increased, but half went toward the war effort, with two years' worth of national income spent on artillery shot away, ships sunk at sea, and supplies abandoned in the jungles of the South Pacific.

In spite of higher nominal income, the standard of living declined. Americans gave up many of life's pleasures: appliances, automobiles, and construction of private housing, and lived with less sugar, coffee, and meat. Yet, during the war, and despite price control and rationing, prices rose an average of 30 percent—with business people fined and jailed for violating price control and rationing regulations. Taxes increased dramatically and permanently. The clear winner in the war was government: it held on to all that taxation and to all its emergency powers. It is why "war is the health of the state" (Randolph Bourne), why permanent revolution is the health of the state (Leon Trotsky): the state keeps its emergency powers by diverting attention away from the fact that spending for war (see government spending in general) lowers the standard of living. [It was price controls during World War II that created our present system of health care: employers circumvented the prohibition on raising wages by offering health insurance.] (For the above facts, see Mark Skousen, *Economics on Trial—Lies, Myths and Realities*, New York, Irwin Professional Publishing, 1991, p. 112.)

9. At the onset of a major financial crisis, to prevent immediate economic collapse, an infusion of cash is necessary. That infusion has no effect on the underlying recession or unemployment rate because that's not what it's for. It's for bailing out the banks. It's for protecting the financial system.

10. Keynesian economics is as much social policy as economic policy. The WPA, for example, was put in place in the

1930s mostly to prevent worker unrest, to keep left-wing intellectuals occupied—keep their minds off overthrowing capitalism. President Roosevelt was worried.

11. When banks were bailed out by government in the 2008 financial crisis, their first thought was to pay off their bad debts, not to loan the money they were given, not to lower interest rates or reduce loan amounts. Rather than stimulate the economy, banks hoarded the money. Why? Because, as suppliers licking their wounds, they were not confident enough. Confidence is the *sine qua non* of a market economy.

Yet during an economic downturn, as part of the market's natural correction process, a favorable thing happens: capital builds up. That creates the perfect opportunity for creative entrepreneurs and private lenders (and the occasional well-run bank) to get together.

The success of a nation depends on the success of its economy, but the success of an economy depends on the nation's producers and entrepreneurs. It does not depend on government; it does not depend on central banks; it does not depend on consumers. The function of a central bank is to keep inflation low, and during a financial crisis to act as lender of last resort; but with Keynesian economics, government becomes a central player, as it also tries to maintain full employment, an impossible task. Why, then, in advanced industrialized nations, aren't leaders of government individuals with vast economic and business experience? Because persons with those qualities are usually so removed from the reality of the lives of working people that they are unelectable. Steve Forbes and Mitt Romney come to mind. Both are business people who grasp the economy, who understand that government should not have thrown so much money at the banks, that too much gas floods the engine—precisely why Quantitative Easing, QE1, QE2 and QE3, had so little effect on employment. If they could find the right candidate, U.S. voters would put a conservative in the White House. However, Forbes' understanding of the economy is still correct: flooding an economy with capital undermines the link between honest work and reward and creates artificial prices—(1) high commodity prices that become a subsidy for countries such as Russia, Venezuela, and the Middle East which depend on natural resources rather than the underlying work of their own people (and use that money to terrorize their own people); (2) high commodity prices that push up the price of farmland, thus, the price of agricultural products; (3) and that inflate profits on Wall Street; (4) housing and sovereign debt price bubbles that lead to an over-extension of both government and private credit; (5) high taxes that take resources from citizens; (6) governments resorting to printing money to pull their nation out of recession. (See Steve Forbes, speech to the Commonwealth Club, 8/24/12, and continuous postings on www.forbes.com.) Stuff all the above into a political sausage to be used at the discretion of government bureaucrats and we have as everywhere in the world countries run by social workers, individuals with political rather than economic skills, instead of business people.

Placing economists in charge would be no better.* Creating dynamism in an economy and assuming entrepreneurial leadership are not what economists do. They analyze economic actions before and after they occur (comparative statics) and look for a pattern. Economists think in terms of scarcity and opportunity cost, that capital invested in one enterprise is no longer available for another. But this is a false zero-sum thought. Market reality is that the industrialized world is awash in capital.** Viable capital projects are what are in short supply—why the New York Stock Exchange is so over-valued, why so much capital worldwide from banks, Quantitative Easing, venture capital, and energy-based sovereign funds chase only a handful of investments. (Privatize a nation's infrastructure, however—roads, bridges, prisons, schools—as public utilities monitored for their profit and performance, and there will be no shortage of funding.)***

*Economists, like social workers, government workers, most politicians such as President Obama, like socialist central planners, *all* liberals, are sociologists at heart—people who would make the world a better place by redistributing income and wealth. What these social engineers do not realize is that taxation does not fall upon the rich, but upon the middle class. When young, middle-class college students do not view redistribution as a taking of money from those willing to work to be given to those not willing to work; by middle age, they do.

One theme of this book is that government cannot tax the rich, that it is only the middle class that pays. [The rich pay something, but negligibly in relation to their wealth or income.] One reason, of course, is that the rich spend more to avoid taxes than governments spend to collect them—as O. J. Simpson beat government prosecutors because he employed his own attorneys, the nation's best and highest paid, so, too, the rich pay their own attorneys, the best, to write and design tax law. The "classic" unscrutinized tax break (rather than industry subsidies which are), is tax forgiveness, for example, the city of San Francisco inducing Silicon Valley corporations to open second offices or, in the case of Twitter's headquarters, by waiving property taxes. Other schemes include special-purpose entities to account for too much income (or too much loss) shown on a federal tax return as an "off balance-sheet" item: Enron, for example, in 2002. Today, Apple, Fiat, and Starbucks employ tax inversion, wherein, respectively, they declare low tax-rate Ireland, Luxemburg or the Netherlands as their home. Governments agree to tax avoidance if, in exchange, it means "job creation;" why governments look the other way with respect to transfer-pricing (transferring or selling goods and services between subsidiaries of multinationals at lower than market price, or at rates that produce better tax treatment in another country—according to *The Economist*, "Corporate Tax Deals, a Bit too Cozy?" 10/4/14, p. 71, firms "reverse-engineering costs attributable to one subsidiary to arrive at a certain level of taxable income with "no economic basis"), or creating stateless subsidiaries (firms incorporated in one country, e.g., Ireland, that have no tax residence).

** Japanese firms hold $2.1 trillion in cash, 44 percent of GDP. Enormous! South Korean firms hold $440 billion, 34 percent of GDP. U.S. firms hold $1.9 trillion, 11 percent of GDP. "Corporate Saving in Asia, a $2.5 Trillion Problem," *The Economist*, 9/27/14, p. 14.

*** What those not in business do not grasp is that "talent attracts capital, not the other way around." Michael Bloomberg, mayor of New York City, affirmed this to Edward Luce in "Rebuilding the U.S. City, *Financial Times*, 6/18/13. Also mentioned was that talent attracts talent, why San Francisco has dramatically changed from a socially and economically diverse city to a highly skilled, highly educated, and highly paid technologically-based monoculture, a population which both attracts and needs its constituents, a natural growth phenomenon that must not be tampered with. This is the beauty of capitalism, what is meant by "creative destruction."

In the early teens, central banks in Europe and the U.S. so flooded the market with money (Quantitative Easing) that interest rates dropped to near zero. Consequently, investors desperate for a higher return purchased ever-riskier stocks, corporate bonds, and real estate rather than low-risk government bonds that pay for infrastructure.

Smart money may already be in the wings. Apple, for one [2014], is taking on huge debt. It sold $13 billion in July and $17 billion earlier in the year (see Fred Norris, "Searching for Yield at Almost Any Price," *New York Times*, Business Days, 2/2/14, p. B-1). Apple has no need for this cash.

The sale of those bonds represents, in fact, an extremely rare economic event—a Giffen good, a good whose price rises as supply rises. That should be a warning to the economy, an economy chasing after anything, because when interest rates rise, eventually the value of bonds will drop. Boom!

Real estate also contributes to new rounds of inflation. To generate business and accommodate subprime borrowers (in reality, most borrowers), lenders drop their credit risk standards

(FICO scores); then, fixed-income investors, pension funds, mutual funds, under obligation to provide a fixed return of more than four percent a year (with short-term U.S. Treasuries paying one-half of one percent, and 30-year Treasuries three percent), chase higher returns from risky investment. Before the 2008 financial crash, pension funds promised an eight percent return. The average discount rate in 1999 had been 7.4 percent, but dropped to 4.7 percent in 2013—meaning that S&P 500 pension obligations of $2 trillion rose to $4 trillion. [Lex Column, *Financial Times*, 7/28/14, p. 12.] As with bonds, if rates drop, price rises. To obtain a higher return, fixed-income investors had two options: extend the maturity of the bonds they had purchased, or, reduce credit quality. Most chose the latter, but there were risks in both: the price of longer-term bonds falls sharply once interest rates rise, and those lower-quality bonds threaten to default. [Fred Norris, *Ibid.*] The higher-than-market returns that investors were achieving were at long-term risk of being wiped out. Certainly, investors who had to sell bonds before their 50-year maturity, pension funds, for example, to make payments to retirees, received less than full value—as happened in Greece, where retirees face half the security they had been led to expect.

[The purpose of this entire endnote is to say that because rates of return are timeless, intervention in the market to improve them is counterproductive.]

12. John Stewart Mill, "The Consumer Theory of Prosperity," *Essays on Some Unsettled Questions of Political Economy* (1830); J. B. Say, "Say's Law, *Traité d'économie politique* (1803); John Maynard Keynes, *The General Theory of Employment, Interest and Money* (1936).

13. Can recessions be prevented? Economists do not have the tools. There are no econometric models to predict or prevent recessions. Consider Alan Greenspan: he did not prick the housing bubble that lead to the 2008 financial crisis. As he said, "maybe it wasn't a bubble; maybe there was a profound underlying change in the world economy." With all the data and tools at his disposal,

Greenspan, as well as most other economists had no idea what was happening. At a Bank of International Settlements conference in 2008, Jagdish Bhagwati, an economist at Columbia University, asked if any of the economists had ever seen a derivative; all replied no. In his 7/31/12 e-mail to me confirming the above, Bhagwati stated that most of the prominent commercial and central bankers at the conference "did not understand the new financial instruments which had precipitated the crisis."

The only possible test of the economy is one that verifies human behavior in relation to pure economic theory—and that has been done. We know through behavioral economics, and now through neuroeconomics, that in any specific situation, human behavior may very well be irrational, but that in general, with respect to marginal utility (how much we value something at the moment), human behavior *is* rational. A question, then, is how can central bankers apply economic theory or econometric modeling to an economic situation that the bankers themselves have never seen? One answer is that such a situation doesn't really exist. Important situations, such as recessions, always exist and are always the same—the result of an over-extension of credit.

It is why game theory is unreliable: it posits hypothetical situations with which the players have no experience. With an unreal situation, one cannot use one's most important decision-making tool, the tool that connects us to the cosmos (and to marginal analysis), *instinct at the moment* (plus real physical and/or financial power at the moment).

Economists and central bankers should not, therefore, run controlled experiments; they are artificial. Lining up real-life examples from the past when problems were supposedly solved and then looking for a pattern is not credible. In 2011, a Nobel Prize in economics was awarded to Christopher Sims and Thomas Sargeant for having developed statistical methods to organize historical data and disentangle the many variables. According to Chris Giles, Martin Sandbu and Claire Jones, "Rational Expectations Theory gets Nobel Nod," *Financial Times*, 10/11/11,

p. 6., their new methodologies are used to figure out whether a policy change that happened in the past affected the economy or whether it was made in anticipation of events that policy makers thought would happen later. The methods also help decipher how regular people's expectations for government policies can affect their behavior.

Nonsense! Such ideas even run counter to contemporary progressivism: governments solving societal problems without regard to the economic consequences, without regard to the practicability of carrying them out, collecting taxes from the rich, for example, under guise of enforcing entitlements regardless of cost—as a mark of civilization.

Sims said that his research was relevant for helping countries decide how to respond to the economic stagnation and decimated budgets left by the financial crisis.

> The methods that I've used and that Tom [Sargent] has developed are central for finding our way out of this mess. But if I had a simple answer, I would have been spreading it around the world.

Hey, when he has the answer, *then*, he should get the Nobel Prize. What is being disingenuously neglected is that even complex economic models deliberately omit some things in order to focus on others. They leave out factors that cannot be modeled satisfactorily, those that might very well produce systemic bias, e.g., large economies, climate change, what F. A. Hayek refers to in his 1945 essay, "The Use of Knowledge," the impossibility of centralizing dispersed knowledge.

Another Nobel economist, James Buchanan, has a better response, namely, that there is nothing to learn from economic modeling. To Buchanan, it is not possible to start with all the information you need, because information is discovered in the process of accumulation. That means that economics is not about analyzing events before they happen, about predicting. Business people do that. *They* are the ones at risk; *they* pay a price if they are wrong. It's not likely that a disengaged, no-skin-in-the-game government bureaucrat will be as focused as someone with everything to lose.

Sims's research, according to the *Financial Times* article cited above, led to a systematic method for distinguishing between unexpected shocks to the economy, such as a sudden change in oil prices, and expected changes. Research using his methodology has helped lend credence to New Keynesianism, the theory that an economy can go into recession because there is not enough demand. That's not New Keynesianism, that's old Keynesianism. As stated, there is nothing government can and therefore should do to reverse a recession. Government can stave off a financial collapse—bail out the banks—but that's all.

But it is Thomas Sargent (along with Bob Lucas) who developed "rational expectations theory," a major idea in modern economics. Yet he did not receive the Nobel for that; instead, it was for his collaboration with Sims. [Perhaps Sims, as president of the American Economic Association, or as a university chair of economics (as per the "Nomination and Selection of Laureates in Economic Science," nobelprize.org), also advises the Nobel selection committee.] Still, even the premise of rational expectations can be questioned. John Kay, in "The Random Shock that Clinched a Brave Nobel Prize," *Financial Times*, 10/8/11, said that the Nobel committee did acknowledge Sargent's contribution to rational expectations theory, the notion that economic behavior depends on expectations about the future, and that economists must consider how such expectations are formed," and acknowledged that the term "rational expectations" is a brilliant linguistic coup. Beyond that, Kay believes the following:

> If the economic world really evolved according to some predetermined model, in which uncertainties are "known unknowns" that can be described by probability distributions, then economists could gradually deduce the properties of this model, and businesses and individuals would naturally form expectations in that light, and that if

they did not, they would be missing obvious opportunities for advantage.

And,

This approach, which postulates a universal explanation into which economists have privileged insight was as influential as it was superficially attractive. But a scientific idea is not seminal because it influences the research agenda of PhD students. An important scientific advance yields conclusions that differ from those derived from other theories, and establishes that these divergent conclusions are supported by observation. Yet as Prof Sargent disarmingly observed, "such empirical tests were rejecting too many good models" in the program he had established with fellow Nobel laureates Bob Lucas and Ed Prescott. In their world, the validity of data and ad hoc adjustments that are usually called "imperfections," it can be reconciled with already known facts —"calibrated". Since almost everything can be explained in this way, the theory is indeed universal; no other approach is necessary, or even admissible. Asked, "do you think that differences among people's models are important aspects of macroeconomic policy debates," Prof Sargent replied: "The fact is you simply cannot talk about their differences within the typical rational expectations model. There is a communism of models. All agents within the model, the econometricians, and God share the same model.

What Kay is saying is that a model that includes all models is not a model (and cannot, therefore, test an hypothesis). Rational expectations theory would be interesting, however, if it meant that government could shock the economy by doing something unexpected, for example, without warning dramatically raise or lower interest rates. Yet, in 1970, the economist Robert Barro put forth an argument against rational expectations theory—that during

163

a recession government spending multipliers will be close to zero precisely because, when government runs a deficit, taxpayers "rationally" add the value of that deficit to their "expectations" of future tax liabilities. (Cited by Andrew T. Young, "Why in the World Are We All Keynesians Again," *Policy Analysis*, Cato Institute, 2/14/13, p. 7.) It is the anticipation of government eventually having to make good on its liabilities that makes consumers increase their savings and decrease their expenditures (perhaps unconsciously acknowledging that a new round of unemployment is just around the corner), which is why Keynesian spending has no effect. The idea is not new: in the 1800s, David Ricardo, in reference to British war bonds, hypothesized that taxpayers would internalize government's intertemporal budget constraints [money today to pay for needs in the future] by decreasing their own expenditures and increasing their own savings. In economics, this undoing of government stimulus is called the Ricardian equivalence. *Ibid*, p. 7.

What about the economy today [2013] in the U.S.? The recession was officially over in 2009, yet output is well below its long-term trend, and unemployment is well above its long-term rate. Policy makers are grappling with this. The Fed has pushed the nation's interest rate on savings down to 0.1 percent, lower than their historical norm of one percent, meaning that monetary policy has reached its limit—meaning that to stimulate the economy, only fiscal policy remains. But with a large federal budget deficit, increased spending and tax cuts are dangerous. The best solution is to keep tax rates as low as possible and cut spending where it would be effective, not in discretionary areas, such as public education and the arts, but in nondiscretionary areas such as Social Security, Medicare and the Pentagon. Reducing a nation's budget deficit equally across-the-board, "sequestration," is mindless and irresponsible. A big cut in Social Security, Medicare and the military, where budgets are unbelievably bloated, would make a difference, would solve the problem. The Keynesian approach of increased government spending is totally irresponsible, as is the populist idea of raising taxes on the rich. Why? Because neither will put a dent in the deficit or the unemployment rate; neither will create economic growth. From the Congressional Budget Office, consider the following projection:

Figure 4
Historical and Projected Ratios of U.S. Debt-to-GDP

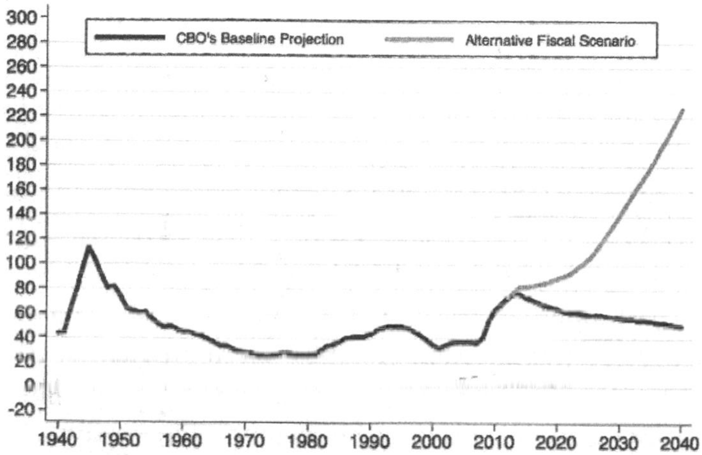

www.cbo.gov 2012 long-term budget outlook (as drawn by Jeffrey Miron, cited below).

U.S. debt in relation to GDP appears to be a sustainable norm, although the nation seems to have no idea how to lower that debt. To lower unemployment with government spending paid for by higher U.S. debt—the vertical gray line—Keynesian fiscal policy, per the graph, is obviously an outrageous solution.

> Thus, the apparent dilemma for policymakers is that what is required to deal with the slow recovery is the opposite of what is required to address the exploding debt. And the "solution" of addressing the recovery, now, via fiscal expansion, and the debt later, via fiscal contraction, is a pipe dream; the "right time" for fiscal contraction will never arrive.

—[Jeffrey Miron (Harvard University), "Should U.S. Fiscal Policy Address Slow Growth or the Debt? A Nondilemma," *Policy Analysis*, Cato Institute, 1/8/13, pp. 4-5.]

After World War II Americans dealt with the red menace—mostly by keeping it at bay. Today Americans must deal with red ink—by keeping it at bay?

14. Alan Blinder, former vice chairman of the Federal Reserve's Board of Governors, "The Case against Discretionary Fiscal Policy," Center for Economic Policy Studies/Princeton University Working Paper No. 100 (June 2004) as cited in Andrew T. Young, "Why in the World Are We All Keynesians Again?" *Policy Analysis*, Cato Institute, 2/14/13, p. 2.

15. The Employment Act of 1946 and The Full Employment and Balanced Growth Act of 1987 committed the federal government to the central goal of full employment. Does that mean that whenever the private sector is not creating full employment, or that the economy is in a state of self-correction, that government should just step in and employ everyone? That's socialism.

What's socialism? Five workers where two are necessary; "any job is better than no job;" social work rather than entrepreneurship. In a mixed economy, socialism requires enforcement of government regulations, with thousands of lawyers and accountants unproductively employed to monitor statutes, with large businesses each spending annually millions of dollars to comply.

What's economic progress? Isn't the disappearance of drudgery, thankless tasks and repetitious work progress? Marx was correct in recognizing problems of alienation, exploitation, and poor working conditions in the labor market, but no system has done more to promote those conditions than communism. Only capitalism promotes opportunity, meaningful work, and high pay.

16. Gains from trade are always possible: As space and time are always relative (theory of relativity), so, too, is value relative (theory of marginal utility). Value of anything is measured in *relation* to how much one already has. It is not absolute; people are not the same. Secondly, there is no such thing as uniformity in production. Firms are not the same; some are more efficient, thus offer lower prices. [Yes, money has replaced barter, but it has not replaced principles of trade. Money is a medium of exchange that represents real goods or services *already* produced, and unless that money is gold, it has no value itself.]

However, according to economist Ronald Coase, trade can be hampered by problems in bargaining—transaction costs of time and energy. This is the classic reasoning why trade is not always possible (and for which, in part, Coase received a Nobel Prize), but to me, a business person, such reasoning does not ring true. California, whose entrenched water rights seem impossible to renegotiate, will, through the courts, eventually resolve that problem. Demanders of drinking water, agricultural water, and environmental protection of water will come to an agreement.

17. Barry W. Poulson, *Economic History of the United States*, (1981) MacMillan Publishing Co., p. 5.

18. The market, with low prices, if not supervised, can destroy a nation's culture and religion: the lure of low prices (precisely what markets provide), virtually a force of nature, can change people's behavior. Just as people in lesser developed nations will cut their rain forests for short-term survival (the low-price solution), people in developed nations (for what they imagine to be the same reason) will cut their culture: work on Sunday, eat fast food, purchase low quality merchandise.

19. Regulation of the economy hurts the creation of new knowledge, itself the product of endless experimentation, failure and destruction of everything that stands in its way.

Regulating the economy because of scarcity of resources, or belief that an economy cannot expand forever, is a false notion: in a free market, high prices ration resources so that resources are always available to firms efficient enough to afford them. To a person in business, as opposed to an economist, scarcity of resources is a non-issue. The real issue is scarcity of viable capital projects. There is *always* an oversupply of capital chasing a minuscule supply of investment opportunity [worldwide, i.e., overpriced stock markets; oversupplied venture capitalists (as concentrated on Sand Hill Road, Menlo Park, California); and oversupplied banks (with $700 billion in deposits from the 2008 financial crisis government bailout—plus deposits from the refinance of real estate as banks loaned the bailout money at government-induced low interest rates and received it back as deposits).] Market reality is that opportunity in business is made, not found. *That* is why there is no solution to world poverty and to the existence of undeveloped nations: not enough entrepreneurs. It does explain why China, a social and political gulag, is an economic powerhouse: lots of entrepreneurs.

[Note: the replication of DNA by 3-D computers will some day reproduce fossil fuels, and that, too, will eliminate scarcity of natural resources. See J. Craig Venter, *Life at the Speed of Light— From the Double Helix to the Dawn of Digital Life*, (2013) Little Brown. So, too, will nuclear energy.]

It is economic growth that creates an ever-increasing standard of living. [Before the Industrial Revolution there was no economic growth because there were no markets: people produced for themselves.] Consider economic growth at 2.3% per year. A family that earns $50,000 a year will see its income increase $1,150 a year. Times 30 years, that's $90,000 a year. In ten generations, that's $1 million a year. Nations, then, should concentrate on economic growth, not on solving social problems. Social problems, the aggregate of individual problems, require short-term relief, not programs that postpone their solution. Social problems are solvable only by individuals themselves: no one can study for you; no one can show up to work for you. [Yes, reduction of a nation's government debt falls inordinately on the backs of the poor, but that is not a reason for nations not to submit to austerity. Reduction of debt will lead to an increase in foreign and domestic investment, thus economic growth, in which the poor inordinately benefit.]

20. Poulson, *Economic History of the United States*, p. 6, cites Adam Smith, *The Wealth of* Nations, Random House Modern Library (1937), Vol. 2 p. 152.

In *The Theory of Moral Sentiments* (1759), which was written before *The Wealth of Nations* (1776), Adam Smith develops the idea of "pursuit of self-interest" (not "selfish interest") as normal human behavior. *The Theory of Moral Sentiments* had such a profound effect in Britain and the American colonies that the publisher was pressured to pre-release the first chapters of *The Wealth of Nations*. The American Framers of the Constitution wanted to incorporate its ideas.

21. One of the primary reasons for creating the United States of America was to provide a free-trade zone across every state. What precipitated the Great Depression, however, was the Smoot-Hawley Tariff (1930), a tariff—the equivalent of a record high tax on more than twenty thousand categories of goods manufactured in the U.S. The tariff triggered a global trade war. Other nations retaliated by imposing high tariffs on *their* imports (U.S. exports). Between 1930 to 1934, the volume of international trade plunged 60 percent. President Hoover and a GOP-led Congress originally placed a high tax on imported goods to protect farmers but expanded it to protect manufacturers. That the tariff war triggered and deepened the Great Depression (coupled with a retraction rather than expansion of the money supply) is, today, a fact undisputed by economists. See John Allison, *The Financial Crisis and the Free Market Cure*, (2013) McGraw-Hill, p. 204. With trade, both parties are better off value for value, win for win. Win-lose, however, according to Allison, in the long run, is not beneficial to the party that wins.

22. Poulson, *Economic History of the United States*, p. 8.

23. *The Federalist Papers, No. 10*, cited in *Ibid*, p. 8.

24. Nations will lose their comparative advantage if their wage rates are not flexible and if their exchange rate is not flexible. That is why Mediterranean countries should not be part of the euro: they lose the ability to devalue their currency [which they need to, often, because of their inherently inefficient culture].

25. Britain has always had the comparative advantage over the U.S. with respect to textile production. Over the last 300 years, the only time U.S. textiles mills were not failing was when they were subsidized.

26. The reason Germany holds the euro together is that the euro's high value makes it difficult for less efficient European nations to compete with Germany. Except, with the euro valued much lower than the Deutsche Mark, Germany, the world's greatest currency manipulator, this time without waging war, has control of the European Union.

27. The tariff on rice in Japan is 778 percent. See "The Gated Globe," *The Economist*, 10/12/13, p. 13.

If Japan, like France, wants to preserve its cultural excellence in the growing and preparation of food, its citizens should be given the choice between knowingly taxing themselves to do so (to subsidize agriculture and restaurants) or paying lower prices (for lower quality).

28. H.D.F. Kitto, *The Greeks*, Pelican Books, England, 1964, p. 100.

29. Peter B. Kenen, *The International Economy*, Fourth Edition, (2000) Cambridge University Press, New York, p. 213.

30. Ibid, p. 213.

31. Ibid, p. 215.

32. Union-driven wage increases outstripped price increases during the window period 1945 to 1975 because there was no competition from Europe, Japan or China. Today, price increase outstrips wage increase.

33. Kenen, p. 221-222.

34. Plato's republic is an example of not giving voters what they want. Plato rejected the idea of government elected directly by citizens-at-large (direct democracy). He favored a republic with leaders drawn from and elected by the aristocracy. This is how it is in communist countries, People's Republics: the communist aristocracy gives citizens what they want, and in exchange, receive the right to make all the rules and to install themselves for life.

35. Consumers will purchase higher-priced imports if the product is better than its domestic counterpart.

36. Gary Clyde Hufbauer and Kimberly Anne Elliott, *Measuring the Costs of Protection in the United States* (Washington, D.C.: Institute for International Economics, 1994), p. 3, as cited in Peter B. Kenen, *The International Economy*, *Op cit*, p. 228. [Although dated, the study is still an important scholarly resource.] Further research by Hufbauer reveals that President Obama's 2009 tariff against China to protect American jobs in tire manufacturing saved a maximum of 1,200 jobs, but cost American consumers higher truck and car prices, in 2011, around $1.1 billion. In that year, the cost per job saved was at least $900,000. See Gary Clyde Hufbauer, "U.S. Tire Tariffs: Saving Few Jobs at High Cost," working paper, http://ideas.repec.org/cgi-bin/htsearch?q=hufbauer+%27US+TIRE+TARIFFS (a research division of the Federal Reserve Bank of St. Louis).

37. Kenen, p. 229.

38. Ibid, pp. 231-232.

39. Ibid, p. 231.

40. Ibid, p. 231.

41. Ibid, p. 231.

42. Ibid, pp. 231 and 233.

Chapter Three

1. William J. Baum and Alan S. Blinder, *Economics: Principles and Policy,* 4th edition, New York: Harcourt Brace Jovanovich, 1988 (as cited in Mark Skousen, *Economics on Trial*; and New York: Irwin Professional Publishing, 1991, p. 185).

2. One must be a business owner to know what it really costs, to know how frustrating it is to deal with the high cost of labor when a nation has a large welfare system as in France, soaking up time and energy spent on dealing with unions, their numerous committees and representatives. Add to that the irresponsibility of politicians with their accumulated *code du travail* (national work rules), plus the irresponsibility of

management (in France): "That's fine in practice, but it will never work in theory."

Consider the situation of Chris Doeblin, owner of the Book Culture bookstores in Morningside Heights near New York's Columbia University, a progressive liberal who has done everything to keep his two community stores open. Customers unabashedly sang his praises. To many, he was a warrior who sustained an intellectual haven for nearly two decades. On June 24, 2014, his workers voted to unionize. Two hours later, he fired all five of them.

The union, Local 1102 of the Retail, Wholesale, and Department Store Union picketed his two stores with giant inflatable rats and urged neighbors to boycott his business. The news spread on Twitter, in local media, and on community email lists ["We'll get him!"].

Doeblin caved in. According to the *New York Times* article, it wasn't that he regretted firing his workers, or that his feelings about unions had changed: "They may have given us the weekend, but they also gave us the mob. My ideology is to make payroll, to make the rent, to make another mortgage payment." Rachel L. Swarns, "Bookstore Owner Takes on a Union, and a Liberal Bastion Takes Sides," *New York Times*, 7/14/14, p. A12.

[Fear of unions seems incongruous for a liberal. Perhaps Chris Doeblin is not a liberal; perhaps his intuition is stronger than his understanding; or he doesn't understand that an employee's weapon is not unionized labor, but the *threat* of unionized labor. The danger of unions is that they force wages higher than market rates (especially when health insurance is included). Unionization can cause a small firm to closes its doors.

One must not confuse this general threat with the window period 1945 through 1975, during which unions successfully caused wages to rise because firms, then, simply raised the price of their products. With Europe and Asia devastated from World War II, there was no competition.

Not true today. Today, worldwide pressure is to lower the price of all products. Where unions are still strong, in France, for example, where wages and benefits are above market, those nations pay dearly. Employers start by not replacing workers when they leave, then replacing them with automation, and finally hiring only temporary workers (at low wages and without benefits). During the economic boom of the early 2000s and the economic recovery of 2014 when the U.S. unemployment rate was four and six percent respectively, France's was 15 percent and among young workers, 25 percent. *That* is the result of unionization: lower employment.

In the U.S. we have the National Labor Relations Act, better known as the Wagner Act, the very purpose of which is to eliminate labor strikes by forcing employers and employees to negotiate. The fact that union membership today is less than ten percent (in the private sector) and at its peak only reached 35 percent in the early 1950s is not proof of failure, but of success: the National Labor Relations Act forced nonunion employers to offer union terms. (See Michael L. Wachter, "The Striking Success of the National Labor Relations Act," *Regulation*, Spring 2014, p. 20.) The implication is that if France should ever reform its labor practices, nonunion workers would receive the equivalent of union benefits.]

[For a quick lesson in labor economics, see John Hicks, *The Theory of Wages*, 1932. Classical economic theory says that wages are one of the factors of production—land, labor, capital—and that the value of any factor is the value of an additional unit of that factor in relation to the revenue that additional unit generates. For a firm barely making a profit, a community bookstore, adding ten percent to the cost of labor will most likely eliminate the firm's profit.

What separates theory from practice, however, is the reality of supply and demand in relation to the factors of production (or the extent to which a firm has a monopoly position in a market). Community bookstores, more sadly, any bookstore, like nonprofit organizations, defy economic analysis. How do they survive? With various grants and loyal high-quality personnel being paid minimum wage.

Do they really defy economic analysis? Doesn't anyone whose livelihood is dependent on balancing the books, who has money at stake, eventually become hard-headed? When forced to make a business decision, especially one that affects the lives of his or her progressive workers, such a decision-maker will be called a capitalist pig. This is as true for nonprofit as it is for for-profit organizations.]

3. Mark Skousen, *Economics on Trial,* New York: Irwin Professional Publishing, 1991, p. 188.

4. Linda Levine, "The U.S. Income Distribution and Mobility: Trends and International Comparisons," Congressional Research Service Report for Congress, 11/29/12.

5. Op cit., p. 189.

6. If social is the opposite of individual (which by definition it is), then social justice is opposed to individual justice and social*ism* is opposed to individual*ism*. Let other countries experiment with socialism, not America. As an international reference, one country should remain free.

The classic economic argument against inequality is that it is simply a byproduct of capitalism's spur to innovation and competition—which is why inequality of income actually *raises* not lowers growth rates. Plus, there is no data to justify the belief that inequality is bad for a nation. Thomas Piketty should study inequality rather than simply line up wealth statistics, declare they show inequality, and recommend redistribution. [See Appendix H, "Thomas Piketty."] Childish concern with numbers displays a liberal Hobbesian fear of social unrest, elitist fear, and lack of respect for the masses. Such concern displays a socialist belief that masses riot because they're poor rather than because, in advanced industrialized nations, they are disconnected from the economy. During the Great Depression, civil unrest did not so much protest poverty or unemployment as demand economic change from capitalism to socialism. It was union-inspired demand for nationalization of industry. In the 1980s, as communism collapsed in the Soviet Union, that idea was finally crushed by Ronald Reagan and Margaret Thatcher. [See Appendix F, "Margaret Thatcher."] Unionization is not something most citizens demand today.*

[Citizens still inclined to demand something from government should ask the Federal Reserve, in addition to monitoring inflation, to monitor inequality and when it reaches a certain level, administer quantitative easing directly to individuals. Polemic? Maybe not. That's what welfare should be: direct cash payment to citizens for short-term relief. Long-term multi-faceted relief impoverishes a nation.

Why? Because citizens weigh the marginal benefit of welfare against its marginal cost and find that the benefit of an untaxed $500 monthly welfare check is worth more than a $600 paycheck, actually more than a $700, even $800 paycheck. When not working one has time to think of other government subsidies for which one might be eligible (or with some planning, become eligible), e.g., housing, child support, or health care. To truly understand the problem of poverty, think in terms of *increasing* poverty. How would you increase poverty? Increase welfare!]

*There *is* a place for unions: to represent workers with respect to salary and working conditions. Employers today try to prevent workers from forming unions by convincing them that the latest in best practices shows that employers' and employees' interests coincide. It's naive for workers to think so—as naïve as it was to let their unions be influenced, in the 1930s, by communists and, in the 1970s, by socialists. Communists used unions to represent *their* political interest in bringing down capitalism in the West. They pushed unions to create social unrest, duped them into demanding above-market wages and nationalization of industry. Once labor caught on, by 1955, union membership dropped from 35 to ten percent of the workforce.

7. Before the Cuban revolution in 1959, Cuba had the most successful economy in Latin America. After the revolution, those responsible for that economy moved to Miami. Today, Cuba's economy is the least successful in Latin America, but might again be the most successful if, like China, the *economic* element of communism gave way to a market economy. Not only would the entrepreneurs in Miami return, but so, too, the entrepreneurialism of all Cubans. [See "The Road Not Taken: Pre-Revolutionary Cuban Living Standards in Comparative Perspective," Marianne Ward and John Devereux, 2010, cited by Wikipedia.]

8. "In fact, it was precisely the inequality of the distribution of wealth that made possible those vast accumulations of fixed wealth and capital improvements which distinguished the age [the nineteenth century] from all others." John Maynard Keynes, *The Economic Consequences of the Peace*, New York: Harper and Row, 1920, p. 19.

9. *Op cit.*, Skousen, p. 194.

10. Joseph Stiglitz, "Inequality Is Holding Back the Recovery," *The New York Times* Opinionator, NYTimes.com, 1/19/13.

11. Bureau of Labor Statistics unemployment rates, bls.gov.

Also, according to a Federal Reserve Survey of Consumer Finances, the wealthiest one percent of Americans held 34.4 percent of the country's wealth in 1965. By 2010, the last year for which data are available, the proportion had barely risen to 35.4 percent. Why do economic writers Thomas Piketty and others worry that inheritance leads to inequality? Also according to Michael Tanner, in "Inequality Myths,": *National Review Online*, 5/14/14, about 80 percent of American millionaires are first-generation. Kevin Williamson of *National Review* (according to Tanner) says that for the richest one percent of Americans, inheritance accounts for just 15 percent of their wealth. That may be a lot of money, but most wealth in the U.S. is earned.

12. Burton Abrams, "Is Inequality Stunting the Recovery?'" *The Washington Examiner*, 2/6/13.

If capitalism played a role in the 2008 financial crisis that plunged many countries into recession and put millions of people out of work (and created inequality), it also played a role in lifting millions of people out of poverty. According to author Devesh Kapur, the most striking beneficiaries are India's Dalits (previously known as the "untouchables"). The Dalits were victimized for centuries in one of the most hierarchical societies in the world. "Capitalism's role in erasing this stain on Indian society is comparable to the contribution it made to curtailing serfdom, feudalism, slavery, and patriarchy in the west." Devesh Kapur, "Western Anti-Capitalists Take Too Much for Granted," *Financial Times*, 7/24/14.

13. Ibid.

14. Congressional Budget Office, "Estimated Impact of the American Recovery and Reinvestment Act on Employment and Economic Output from January 2012 through March 2012," May 2012.

Handing out money to save freedom is insurance: freedom is not free. Those who do not like the idea of economic freedom—who do not realize (or believe) that social, political and economic freedom are inherently interconnected, that the degree to which you suppress one, you suppress the other two—have to be accommodated, paid off, just as unstable regions in the world must be accommodated.

[However, we have let the state grow too large. The Leviathan has grown because no one cares to stop it; no one knows who's paying. The rich and the poor aren't paying. It is the middle class who pays most of the nation's taxes, although to compensate, even *they* eventually demand higher wages. (Ask a salaried person how much he or she earns, and they'll state their after-tax earnings: "All I want to know is how much I take home.") In other words, the world is exactly how it would be if there were no taxes at all, except poorer. Why? Because the world is unnecessarily paying for the services of a third party, government, to do things individuals should do for themselves. Health care, for example, would cost less if, without intermediaries, Medicare, Medicaid, employer's tax-deductible insurance policies, the two parties, doctors and patients, would negotiate price and service between themselves. Public education, if provided by the private sector, would cost less. With income tax refunded, few parents would not send their children to school. Originally, public education (thanks to Thomas Jefferson, whose reasoning was that democracy for its own preservation needs an educated public) was created for those who could not afford schooling. The state provided the funds, but did not operate the schools. (Then, as now, the funds were supplied through property taxes—fair, even progressive, in that property taxes are proportionate to the dollar value of the land, which means that people in poorer neighborhoods pay less. The landlord may write the check, but it's always the tenant who pays.)]

15. Op cit.

16. Skousen, p. 199.

17. However, in 2012, the savings rate in Japan was 1.9%, 4.3% in the U.S. See household saving rates in OECD countries, *Global Finance Magazine* online at www.gfmag.com.

18. Op cit., p. 201.

19. Ibid, p. 201.

20. The free market is capable of solving all societal problems, but that does not mean at a particular moment in time that it will. Sometimes it's necessary for government to push the private sector, and if the private sector does not come through, step in on its behalf. That is because timing, the heart of business transactions, is also at the heart of government intervention. Alan Greenspan, for example, chose not to step in to burst the real estate bubble that caused the 2008 financial crash.

Government might step in to avert a nationwide financial crisis, even nationalize those industries it bails out (provided those industries are allowed to buy themselves back at a price that amply reimburses taxpayers), but the process should be quick: in and out; not five years of quantitative easing.

A word of caution: economics is about trade, the trade and trade-offs that individuals make. Which means that in a free society, outside of a major crisis, government has no part in the economy. Social, political and economic actions are so interrelated that there is no act of economic intervention that will not affect social and political relations.

[Note: the standard definition of economics is wrong: that economics is about scarce resources. Resources are not scarce; they are for the taking. As long as there is competition, price rises until only the most efficient suppliers obtain them, those who will not waste them. Scarce resources is a static notion that does not capture the production process in a market economy. Such an idea does not capture reality, that there is always a dearth of viable capital projects, why the world's major banks all have enormous deposits on hand; why, worldwide, real interest rates are near zero; why venture capitalists take on so many projects. (Most are not viable, one out of ten is.)

An example of government intervention in the economy is rent control. Rent control allows a tenant to tell his landlord exactly how much rent he will pay, rather than the other way around. What are the consequences? Perhaps none, because rent control is a symptom of a deeper government intervention, no-growth public policy that keeps the supply of housing less than the demand. The consequence pushes the price of housing so high that it creates windfall profit for landlords far in excess of their loss due to rent control. For reasons of nostalgia, of keeping a city looking exactly as it was in 1900, cities such as San Francisco forget the principle reason they exist in the first place: to facilitate commerce. Those who came to market-towns to sell their produce, tired of commuting, built apartments over their stores and stayed. That is still true. Tired of commuting, people want to live in the city where they work.

Yet planners in much of California, instead of advocating that towns and cities build vertically as do metropolitan areas everywhere else in the world, facilitated horizontal construction—

asphalting the entire region with housing and freeways. Those planners allowed cutting down orchards and paving over the world's richest soil deposit, Santa Clara Valley—today, Silicon Valley. (Adding to nostalgia, planners advocate that commuters ride their bicycle or take public transportation, counter-cultural anti-business solutions that hinder the flow of cars and trucks, commerce, and that push cities into accommodating residential rather than commercial needs.]

21. As part of the Soviet cultural evolution, thousands of thousand-year-old villages were destroyed, with the people dispersed.

22. Dialectical materialism, that everything is material and that change takes place through the struggle of opposites, is the official philosophy of communism. It is sometimes called historical materialism, which is a better term, because it says directly that social, political and intellectual life reflect the underlying economic structure, that human beings create forms of social life solely in response to economic needs. Many economists agree, at least with the material part. But the struggle, the dialectic, is not correct. That idea, as applied by Hegel—struggle through thesis, antithesis, and synthesis—is true to the extent that all learning is trial and error (evolution of the species, for example), but as applied by Karl Marx is not true. Marx's economic system of communism is as false as was Ptolemy's system of science (which lasted 1,000 years), that the sun revolves around the earth.

23. Regulation that tells banks not to cheat or lie is not regulation; it's the pathetic reaction of noneconomist politicians running for office on populist platforms, unaware that businesses cannot survive if they operate fraudulently. Attorneys see to that.

24. Average daily turnover in derivatives grew an unprecedented 69% to $3.2 trillion from April 2004 to 2007, and grew again to $3.98 trillion, in 2010. Impose government regulation and investors will switch to another investment vehicle. See Bank of International Settlements, "Triennial Central Bank

Survey – Foreign Exchange and Derivatives Market Activity, 2007 and 2010," online at bis.org/statistics.

25. The Dickensian hell of factory conditions at the start of the Industrial Revolution (upon which Marx based all his writings), actually replaced winter starvation in unheated dirt floor cottages with the warmth of the factory, and, for the first time, some education for children.

The Industrial Revolution brought an enormous increase in standards of living. The main reason that some people think they still live in poverty, in industrialized countries, is that they are not content with relative wealth (running water, heat, solid shelter, food, clothing); they want absolute wealth. In the U.S. and Europe, such absolute wealth has become an absolute right. Consequently, people are trapped with rent or mortgage payments way over their heads.

26. The closer a country is to true communism, the closer it is to death by starvation: Russia 1931-33 (eight million), China 1958-61 (30 million), North Korea 1994-98 (two to three million, estimated).

27. In 1963, GDP per capita in Ghana was $179; in South Korea it was $82 per capita (*Financial Times*, "Lunch with the FT: Ha-Foon Chang," 11/30/13). In 2012, GDP per capita in Ghana was $2,047; in South Korea, $30,801 (World Bank 2005-2012, per Wikipedia).

28. Marx never set foot in a factory or ever talked to a business owner. [Friedrich Engels inherited wealth from his family's textile mills, but did not build or operate a factory himself. (Like Marx, because of his revolutionary writings, he was constantly on the run from the law.) Engels relied upon his childhood memories of factory conditions.] To invent socialist economic theories requires that this be so. Similarly, those who reject values and discipline of the material world, beatniks, hippies, tribal people, and liberals, who advocate solving economic problems through the political process, have the force of their social and political opinions strengthened precisely by their

ignorance of economics, just as when a person missing one faculty, sight, has the other four senses, hearing, taste, touch, smell (plus intuition) strengthened.

A liberal intellectual will acknowledge the beauty in mathematics but not in economics, the beauty in art but not in business; he or she will acknowledge that in life all things are interconnected, except in business, because one's not supposed to like and therefore understand business, or assumes, because one business behaves badly, that all businesses behave badly—a very un-Zen approach to life, the refusal to reconcile unpleasant opposites. So certain are liberals in their beliefs in communism or socialism, so elite in their progressivism, they have (or had) no hesitation in advocating, by violent means if necessary, a total change in how society is organized—in the case of China and the Soviet Union, the murder of 60 million citizens; in the case of Germany and Japan, fascism, socialism from the right, another 60 million.

The idea that it would be better not to organize society at all does not enter their minds. The idea that socialist governments chase their entrepreneurs out of the country, as enemies, does not enter their minds.

29. Unlike the French Revolution, the collapse of the Soviet Union was not violent. In the Soviet Union, both the proletariat and the aristocracy were starving; both agreed to end it. [Under capitalism, man exploits man. Under communism, it's just the opposite.]

30. We don't know the future of China. Karl Marx never intended agricultural societies to turn to communism. Marx believed that capitalism is the necessary first step toward industrializing an agricultural economy.

From the 1950s through the 1970s, until Deng Xiaoping, China made the mistake of trying to skip the capitalist step. China, now, knows that its population must first own the means of production and their own homes. *Then* China can take the jump into communism and confiscate that new wealth. Are we misreading the leashed freedom that China allows its citizens, not only in Hong Kong, but probably some day in Taiwan?

We are with respect to Turkey. Turkey is hiding its return to Islam from the world. One reading on this might be, as the Turkish economy slows [2014], takes on government debt ostensibly to bolster the economy and does nothing to prevent citizens from living beyond their means, that the Turkish government is encouraging a crash, after which it will step in with an Islamic state.

With both Turkey and China, the clue will be capital flight. If things go wrong, it will not be because foreign speculators pulled their money out, but because well-informed locals were the first to flee.

31. Economic growth is the real solution to poverty, but is there a limit to growth? Absolutely not. Neither is there a limit to resources. There may be a limit to water and topsoil, but there is no limit to technology. Israel blooms because of technology: they desalinate the ocean. America blooms because of technology: two percent of the nation, its farmers, using only a fraction of the land, produce enough food to feed the world.

With economic growth the solution, why is there still discussion about redistribution of wealth? Market reality is that the forces of supply and demand direct the largest portion of a nation's wealth to those already wealthy. The extent to which that is windfall or a market quirk, society might consider redistribution— except that another market reality is that the total of all windfall and excess income is not nearly enough to solve the nation's needs. Redistribution through taxation is not a solution.

Plus, government can never raise enough money from the rich. Multibillionaire George Soros, a liberal in favor of taxation of the rich, in 2011, closed his famous hedge fund Quantum Funds to nonfamily members. The reason: to avoid regulatory scrutiny under Dodd-Frank. See "George Soros Picks Up $5.5 Billion as Quantum Endowment Fund Soars," *Financial Times*, 2/9/14. [Note also that the fund is based in Curaçao (formerly Netherlands Antilles) and in the Cayman Islands.]

Not only does the market steer most wealth to those already wealthy, but so, too, does market regulation. Sarbanes-Oxley and Dodd-Frank are so expensive that only the largest firms can comply—meaning that if small firms do not shut down, they will merge with the large: how monopolies are born.

Taxation is regulation. With the U.S. corporate tax rate the highest in the world, 39 percent [2016], U.S. multinationals respond to such regulation by moving their assets offshore. Apple's tax inversion (and debt accumulation) as a means of lowering taxes is the perfect example. (See Chapter 2, "Timeless Rates of Return," endnote *11*, paragraphs six and nine.) Funds are rerouted to render them stateless. The tax savings, an unfair competitive advantage, are then used to buy up the competition. Large firms use the "tax dividend" to offer more money for those smaller firms than they are worth. Stockholders accept, and again, monopolies are born. [Should nations eliminate high personal and corporate taxes, wealthy individuals and multinationals would repatriate their earnings. All 602 banks in the Cayman Islands would close.]

32. Robert E. Lucas, Jr., Consultant, "The Industrial Revolution: Past and Future," Federal Reserve Bank of Minneapolis, 2003 Annual Report Essay, last paragraph, www.minneapolisfed.org/publications/the-region/the-industrial-revolution-past-and-future.

33. Victor Hugo once stated that the law in France is fair: even the wealthy are forbidden from sleeping under bridges at night.

So, too, is law in the Bible fair: everyone pays ten percent. Nowhere is it mentioned that if your crops fail you give nothing or that if you have a bumper crop you give triple tithe. *Unfair* is one person paying one rate, one person paying another.

34. Understood at the time of the Constitutional Convention, 1787, and stated clearly by James Madison in *Federalist Paper 51* (referring to the need for "separation of powers") is that, "If men were angels, no government would be necessary," but there is still the problem of protecting citizens *from* government—from government reprisal, for example, from the Governor of New Jersey, in January 2014, closing two out of three lanes of a freeway entrance during rush hour for the purpose of tying up traffic for hours.

However, not understood at the time, with socialism not yet even a notion, was that those who benefit from taxation are the ones who choose the rates. That is what entitlements and dictatorship of the proletariat are all about—although it was necessary for socialism to run its course for the proletariat to finally learn that it was never the rich, but *they*, who paid.

35. $1.5 trillion would be enough if most poor were not living in expensive urban areas. Why should the nation subsidize, or worse, build substandard low-income housing in beautiful cities such as San Francisco and New York, when, in fact, so many cities are tearing down original primary residences, as in Detroit?

[Why do we underestimate the poor? Society should admire those who find a way to get out of paying taxes.]

The poor are not stupid. I had a tenant, a welfare mom living in a renovated two-bedroom Victorian apartment in San Francisco. Her three children, spaced over five-year intervals, enabled her for many years to receive Aid for Families with Dependent Children (AFDC, which now has a different name because government regularly changes the names of its welfare programs to obscure from the public that the programs are never eliminated), Section 8 housing vouchers, food stamps, Medicaid, and health care for her children. For extra spending money, she rented her bedroom to a working woman (her mother!) by the hour.

And the rich are not stupid. Because American corporations are taxed both on their national and international earnings, many give up their American citizenship to incorporate overseas. Apple recently incorporated in Ireland. Or they buy 20 percent of a foreign firm and call that a cross-border merger, a "tax inversion," in order to pay tax abroad at a lower rate. Those firms keep their

185

foreign earnings overseas and borrow domestically when they need cash. Why pay a 39 percent repatriation fee (when corporate income is taxed at 12.5 percent in Ireland)?

That's why Wall Street exists—for the wealthy to find ways to avoid paying taxes. Barclays and Deutsche Bank developed "basket options" (for which, in 2014, they were under Senate investigation)—high-leverage-derivative options based on a basket of underlying assets of commodities, securities and currencies, which, if the options are exercised after one year, are treated as long-term capital gains. Twenty-five percent is better than 35 percent.

Our lives are limited by the human condition: a combination of responsibility and carelessness in which business, tempted with fraud, needs regulation (a game of cops and robbers: government changes the law, Wall Street changes the theft); in which Middle Eastern politics, tempted to blow up innocent civilians, needs monitoring (a game of tit-for-tat: one side launches a rocket, the other side launches it back).

These problems have no solution. Yet, they must be managed. The world desires peace among nations, honesty among people, but if religion is not replaced with science and government with individual responsibility, the world cannot change.

The Age of Reason, the Enlightenment, produced a great political document, the U.S. Constitution. That was possible because its framers separated church and state, government and individual. The Constitution could not be written today: progressives and religious fundamentalists would prevent it— prevent anyone resembling the Founding Fathers from even attending the Convention:

> Whenever we read the obscene stories, the voluptuous debaucheries, the cruel and tortuous executions, the unrelenting vindictiveness, with which more than half the Bible is filled, it would be more consistent that we call it the word of a demon than the word of God. It is a history of wickedness that has served to corrupt and brutalize…

My religion is to do good. My own mind is my own church.

—Thomas Paine

Religious controversies are always productive of more acrimony and irreconcilable hatreds than those which spring from any other cause...

—George Washington

(Refused to take communion, to kneel in prayer in churches (or at Valley Forge), have a priest at his deathbed or take last rites.)

The government of the United States is not in any sense founded on the Christian religion.

—John Adams, at the signing of the Treaty
of Tripoli, 1797

The above quotes were printed in the *New York Times*, July 4, 2013, in a one-page ad entitled "Celebrate our Godless Constitution," paid for by the Freedom From Religion Foundation.

In other words, allowed to attend the Convention today would be those who agree with the following:

It's going to be very, very exciting. [Congress has] to pass the bill [the Affordable Care Act] so that you can find out what is in it, away from the fog of controversy.

—Nancy Pelosi, March 9, 2010, at the Legislative
Conference for the National Association of Counties.

Pelosi's reasoning is that of a communist revolutionary: Communism is going to be very, very exciting. We have to overthrow capitalism so we can find out what's in it, away from the fog of opposition. (We can't wait for the masses to vote for it: they just don't understand.)

This is the same reasoning behind Pelosi's notion that Republican-led efforts to rein in government are pointless, because there is nothing left to cut.

> The cupboard is bare. There are no more cuts to make. It's really important that people understand that.

—Nancy Pelosi, Interview broadcast on CNN's "State of the Union (cited by *Washington Times* 9/22/13

The federal budget has doubled in size over 12 years, from $1.9 trillion in 2001 to $3.8 trillion in 2013.

There's nothing to cut?

36. Putting a Face on America's Tax Returns, edited by Scott A. Hodge, Tax Foundation, Washington, D.C., 2013, p. 2.

37. Ibid, p. 2.

38. Ibid, p. 10.

39. Ibid, p. 11.

40. Ibid, p. 44.

41. Ibid, p. 17.

42. Ibid, p. 50. Even if citizens receive services from government that they would have paid for anyway—education, childcare, healthcare, Social Security—that is not an excuse for socialism. There is no excuse for an inefficient third party, government, to waste half the revenue it receives administering programs that have no chance of success. Look at socialized Sweden, 1930 to 1990, where well-meaning wealthy citizens gave it a try.

43. Can tax rates be lowered by closing loopholes and increasing government regulation of business? Of course, but why is the Volcker Rule [first adopted December 2013 as part of Dodd-Frank, to restrict speculative investing by U.S. banks] such a good idea, when it may cause banks to fail?

For example, in 2014, Zions Bank, a large regional bank, like many businesses—banks, insurance companies, publicly held corporations like Enron in 2002—hid its losses from public view, placing them in footnotes to its financial statements as "special purpose entities," as projects created specifically to account for company losses. Yes, Sarbanes-Oxley, Dodd-Frank, the Volcker Rule, all try to eliminate this kind of nontransparent accounting, but why can't the accounting profession do that? Why should a Zions Bank be forced to sell off securities at a loss (rather than waiting for the market to rebound), or to raise capital by selling additional stock (and dilute the stock's value to previous owners), solely to accommodate new rules for transparency? Why can't government prosecute for fraud, but beyond that, stay away?

Consumers (by withdrawing their funds) and prosecuting attorneys keep markets in check. Zions Bank (like Enron) created loans *to itself*—collateralized debt obligations (CDOs), with those by Zions Bank secured by Trust Preferred Securities—without tangible assets to back them. Why won't the market catch up with that? The bank issued notes for the purpose of making the bank appear to be well capitalized, worth AAA ratings, qualifying for interest payments claims as tax deductions. Later it labeled those Trust Preferred Securities as equity, stock, so that when Zions didn't want to make an interest payment, it could simply suspend payment for up to five years. Whoa! If markets accept such behavior, markets deserve to lose. Floyd Norris reminds us, in "Loophole Slowly Tightens on a Bank," *New York Times*, 12/20/13 (from which the above analysis of Zions Bank was taken), *"Oh what a tangled web we weave, when first we practice to deceive."*—Sir Walter Scott.

[On January 14, 2014, federal regulators bent to the will of the banking industry and revised the Volcker Rule to eliminate community banks such as Zions. See Mathew Goldstein, "Regulators Ease Volcker Rule Provision Smaller Banks," *New York Times*, 1/15/14. There it is, then: Wall Street helping markets go around unnatural government interference. Always the case, which is why business is indifferent to regulation: business asks only that government not change regulations so often. With continual change, businesses cannot plan, and if they cannot plan, capital projects are postponed and if capital projects are postponed, employment is postponed. And business is indifferent to being fined: fines are already accounted for as a reoccurring expense. The SEC should do as the Department of Motor Vehicles (whose fines do not seem to control bad driver behavior): give points for infractions of the law, and when a certain total is reached, take away the license.]

The question is still: can tax rates be lowered by closing loopholes? Not when government provides so many tax deductions. The *real* question: why should government, a neutral third party whose sole function is to protect civil liberties, subsidize any business? Why should government subsidize energy savings, the installation of solar panels, for example? That's social policy. It's political policy: populism, giving voters what they want without telling them that they (and not the rich) are going to pay for it. What happened to the classical economic understanding that citizens, through the market, through the goods and services they choose to purchase, automatically pursue best social policy?

44. Steve Forbes, "Summary of Steve Forbes' Flat Tax Plan" (1995). www.pbs.org/newshour/bb/congress/forbes_flat_tax.html

45. A flat tax is progressive to the extent that it allows normal deductions for business, payroll, for example. After those deductions, it is marginally flat. Such a tax is called a "marginal" flat tax. A "true" flat tax allows no deductions.

46. The U.S. is the only nation in the world in which half the population is good (liberals) and half bad (conservatives). Most of the world is 90 percent "good." (The UN!)

47. To people in India, overweight Americans living in private homes with hot and cold running water are not poor.

48. David F. Friedman, *Price Theory: an Intermediate Text*, 2nd edition, (1990) South-Western Publishing, Livermore, CA, p. 500.

49. Taxing the rich at a higher rate is not unfair, but how much more tax is there to obtain from the rich?

According to Richard Epstein, a legal scholar and lecturer at the University of Chicago Law School, "Today the United States collects more money in income tax from the top one percent of earners than from the bottom 95 percent of taxpayers. Ouch."

See Richard A. Epstein, *Design for Liberty*, (2011) Harvard University Press, p. 108.

50. The Statute of Frauds, 1677, makes it illegal to transfer real property without a written contract.

Thus, the first step in negotiation is to obtain a contractual right to acquire the asset. Only then will the purchaser have equal footing with the owner (who now needs the buyer to release him from the contract). [Owners of assets, property, should never sign contracts unless presented contingency-free.]

And then, price is not the only object of negotiation. Leverage is just as important. With 100 percent leverage (zero dollars down), there is no limit to the size of a purchase—$4 million, $40 million, $400 million.

51. Firms that issue publicly traded assets, stocks, for example, are, by law, required to issue accompanying financial statements—a major reason, besides having to comply with onerous government regulation, why firms do not go public: politically motivated legislation and tax codes (such as Sarbanes-Oxley and Dodd-Frank) make company owners and directors vulnerable to presenting fraudulent financial statements at every stockholder meeting. The only reason a privately held firm would go public would be to finance projects for which no bank will make a loan. But when firms go public to cover the fact that their projects are risky, *caveat emptor*.

Corporations pay their accountants, rating agencies and investment analysts to provide favorable reviews. (Favorable reviews are the price accountants, rating agencies, and investment banks pay a corporation to obtain relevant information—without which they cannot operate.) Financial statements of publicly held corporations are, thus, a lie. But then, in business and politics, so, too, is the truth. Obamacare, Medicare, Social Security, set up to be self-sustaining in their early years, were always understood by Congress to create debt in their later years: everyone participated in these fictions. Social Security, for example, created in 1935 during the Great Depression to provide relief for those over 65, issued its first payment in 1941—no help during the Depression—and with the knowledge (from actuarial tables at the time) that average life-span was 60, hoped actually to pay nothing at all (and that if people in the future had longer life spans, that was their problem). [U.S. unfunded debt, most of which is Medicare and Social Security (which will increase with Obamacare), is $103 trillion (December 2019). See JUST FACTS, http://wwwjustfacts.com/nationaldebt.asp.]

Now, Americans have to pay down their national debt, and, like Europeans, accept real austerities. One solution is progressive taxation: those in lower income brackets would pay 50 percent; those in higher brackets, 70 percent. The French already do this. The U.S. never will: Americans know that you cannot tax the rich. Instead, the U.S. will cut its national budget by mindlessly cutting everything at the same rate: sequestration.

52. Price serves the same intertemporal function. For example, the price of health care in the U.S. is three times what it should be (the reason for the Affordable Care Act), which indicates that demand for health care far exceeds its supply (although, in the Bay Area, for example, hospitals are one-half empty and physicians have less than full caseloads). Something, then, is seriously wrong with the market. With the advent of Medicare and Medicaid in 1965, along with, in 1949, employer tax write-offs for employee health insurance premiums, and the illegality of purchasing health insurance across state lines [in violation of U.S. Constitution Article 1, Section 8 which forbids restrictions on interstate commerce], health insurance devolved into pre-paid health care rather than insurance—in which demand, paid by government, increased three-fold. And consumers were completely removed from price negotiation. That's not sustainable. Should citizens ever reject socialized health care, the free market for health care that existed before 1965 would return, a time when health insurance, auto insurance, property insurance, and life insurance all cost the same, about $200 a month in today's dollars.

53. "Stern Review on the Economics of Climate Change," (2006) HM Treasury, Cabinet Office, Great Britain, Cambridge University Press.

54. Indur M. Goklany, "Discounting the Future," *Regulation* (Spring 2009), pp. 36-40.

Chapter Four

1. Neutrality is at the heart of the U.S. Constitution. Neutrality means that fairness has to do with rules, not outcomes, that justice is about process, not end-states. Yes, at its inception, African-Americans, unfairly, were not counted as full persons, but it was understood that later they would use the Constitution to reverse that injustice. In other words, in 1787, to induce all 13 states to agree to the Constitution, the Founding Fathers were willing to say or do almost anything.

They understood the importance of the document. They knew a major source of the world's problems is that nations do not live by sets of rules to which their citizens have agreed, and that without government neutrally enforcing those rules, citizens will take the law into their own hands: in the twentieth century with European and East Asian fascism and communism; today, the Middle East, Africa and Latin America, where powerful individuals surrounded by private armies intimidate whomever they want.

Consider what went into making the U.S. Constitution: (1) The heritage of 5th Century Athens [the greatest civilization that ever existed, where *every* citizen (male) had the opportunity publicly to defend his position (and in the most sophisticated language ever, ancient Greek, a language that forced speakers logically to prepare their thoughts before speaking or else fail to be understood—see H. D. F. Kitto, *The Greeks*), and was given the opportunity to vote on every issue, which did eliminate jury bias.]

With such careful preparation of language, however, came demagoguery, and with a population explosion, the unmanageability of direct democracy. After a brief 100 years, with Athens increasingly corrupt, that high moment in world history—for philosophy, art, literature, mathematics, science, and government —came to an end.

(2) The legacy of seventeenth and eighteenth century Age of Enlightenment in which Greek and Roman law were coupled to social, political and economic thought that emerged in England, Scotland, France, and America. This featured Francis Bacon, Thomas Hobbes, John Locke, David Hume, Adam Smith, and Montesquieu. Bacon (who studied Machiavelli, who advocated reliance not on the aristocracy, vain and disloyal, but on the masses who, if given a measure of social, political and economic freedom, would be so grateful *they* would support the prince, all of which is *the* root of democracy) held that "progress" (from the stagnant European Middle Ages) was possible by applying the technology of the day and by applying the "scientific method' to every idea, i.e., verify before applying (not done in 1917 with Russian communism); Hobbes thought that man in a state of nature is brutal, that it was necessary first to create a Leviathan (big government), then, allow some personal freedom within that overarching net; Locke said the opposite, from nature itself man derives his freedom, thus, the right to one's life, liberty and property is *natural law*, and by extension the sole purpose of government is to protect that freedom; Smith (whose thoughts incorporate those of Hume and Locke) argued that if everyone pursued his or her own interest and as a consequence became dependent upon each other (also, as a result of the division of labor) that invisibly, spontaneously, the market would organize society better than anything man could possibly design. Finally, Montesquieu, to prevent an individual or the state from becoming too powerful, advocated political power be separated into branches of government. All of this James Madison incorporated (almost single-handedly) into the U.S. Constitution, the greatest political

document ever created. [To appreciate what the Founding Fathers created, what Alexis de Tocqueville understood, the beauty of 5th century Athens, read Thucydides "Pericles' Funeral Oration"—and be shocked: that's us!]

2. If the world supply of oil is lowered, but demand remains constant, its price will rise. That's how markets work. With long-run rates of return timeless, markets guarantee that windfall profits are later countered by unexpected losses.

Markets are impersonal, although decisions about trade are not. Decisions are subjective—made by individuals—based on marginal utility, on supply on hand *at the moment*. Trade cycles, thus, are a response to aggregate change in individual marginal utility. Still, according to the great economic thinker, Knut Wicksell, trade cycles are only secondary, a response to a change in commodity prices. [See Knut Wicksell, *Lectures on Political Economy*, Volume Two, (1950, first published in 1935), Routledge & Kegan Paul Ltd., London, p. 209.] From the perspective of Austrian economics, which places man at the center of all economic activity, it's not important that investors are not always rational, that as human beings they cannot help falling prey to dangerous nearsightedness, to forgetting that high prices lead to more supply. According to Wicksell, in the heat of a boom, this dynamic is forgotten (*ibid*). At the height of the last trade cycle, 2007, housing prices soared, although the U.S. has an almost unlimited capacity to build.

3. Creating panic during the Eurozone crisis was, in part, an act by Germany to divert attention from the fact that it is the largest currency manipulator in the world. As mentioned, Germany keeps the euro undervalued (by at least 30 percent), the real reason behind high German exports and low unemployment. See Robin Jackson, ADR Enterprises, England, in "Letters," The Economist, 4/6/13. Germany will never let the euro crash. Germany will always bail out failing eurozone nations.

4. In the U.S., the use of imported intermediate components is about ten percent of production, but in OECD countries, about 25 percent

(see Shimeli Ali and Uri Dadush, "Trade in Intermediates and Economic Policy," Carnegie Endowment for International Peace, 2/9/11, www.voxeu.org/article/rise-trade-intermediates-policy-implications#fn1).

When the cost of the components of production is higher than market, when, for example, labor is so inefficient that production takes too much labor, producers cannot compete on world markets unless the nation devalues its currency. By joining the European Union, inefficient Greece lost that option.

5. Citizens should beware their wishes as there's always a chance they'll come true—along with their unseen consequences. In 1965, before government intervened in the health care market with Medicare and Medicaid, the cost of health insurance was about the same as auto insurance, property insurance, and life insurance. Unseen was that interference would cause demand to increase, consumers to be removed from the process of bargaining over price, and health insurance to transform into pre-paid health care, in other words, that it would cause the price of health care to rise. Today, health insurance costs three times that of auto insurance, and with our current attempt at universal health care, Obamacare, it will rise again. In mid-2013, front-end early savings expired and back-end scheduled increases began.

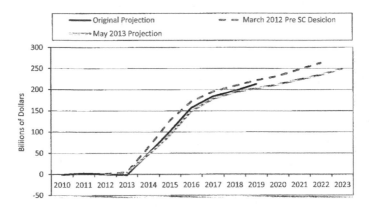

Source: Congressional Budget Office, "Effects on Health Insurance and the Federal Budget for the Insurance Coverage Provisions in the Affordable Care Act—May 2013 Baseline," May 14, 2013, http://www.cbo.gov/sites/default/files/cbofiles/attachments/44190_EffectsAffordableCareActHealthInsuranceCoverage_2.pdf; Congressional Budget Office, "Updated Estimates for the Insurance Coverage Provisions of the Affordable Care Act," March 13, 2012, http://www.cbo.gov/sites/default/files/cbofiles/attachments/03-13-Coverage%20 Estimates.pdf; Congressional Budget Office, "H.R. 4872, Reconciliation Act of 2010 (Final Health Care Legislation)," March 20, 2010, http://www.cbo.gov/sites/default/files/cbofiles/ftpdocs/113xx/doc11379/amend reconprop.pdf.

Yes, mandatory universal health insurance would lower overall cost, but not within a system that's half-government and half-free. Health care either should either be converted to a government monopoly or be set free. The middle road is not acceptable. Unfortunately, no political party anywhere in the world espouses such a radical solution. In the U.S., the conservative argument against universal health insurance is simply that in a free society governments do not force citizens, as a price of citizenship, to purchase goods and services. The liberal argument is that universal health insurance is another tax, not something citizens need to be concerned about. Ya want insurance, Call 1-800-FREE-LUNCH.

Karl Marx's wish, for which he thought there would be no negative consequences, was for the nationalization of the means of production (the most absolute government intervention). And he got it, although immediately, Frédéric Bastiat, a nineteenth century French political economist, provided the classic counterargument, namely, that socialists are not accounting for what is not seen, that money directed to where it would not go ordinarily, a baseball stadium rather than to new clothing, creates enormous economic inefficiency. [Were it not backed by its own natural resources, the Soviet Union would have collapsed within a few years. Ditto, Cuba —which survived on those same resources. Today, on Venezuela's resources.]

6. National budget deficits (borrowing to stay alive) exist because revenue from taxation is insufficient to pay the nation's expenditures. In the U.S., with neither the rich nor poor paying taxes (tax law and accountants see to that), it's not the fault of the IRS. Consider the preamble to the IRS "1040" tax form, in 1962 when, at age 16, I filed my first return. It had the stand-alone phrase, "Read these instructions carefully; do not pay more than you are required."

The fault is populist politicians who promise goods and services at public expense without providing the means to pay. Afraid to ask middle-class voters to pay higher taxes, they simply yell, "Tax the rich!" That is why budget deficits have become a permanent part of contemporary democracy. In the European Union, the Maastricht Agreement limits nations to a budget deficit of no more than three percent. What's wrong with no deficit? The argument in Europe, however, is not about the immorality of permanent deficit, but about the total arbitrariness of such a limit. In Europe, no one is saying that borrowing is really tax evasion, that the evaded amount will be paid in the future by nonvoting younger and future generations, and that those future generations [like Greece today] will pay higher taxes, receive lower amounts of government assistance, experience currency inflation and probably sovereign bond defaults. There is no debate because no one questions this: politicians installing stoplights at intersections to collect tax from motorists to pay motorists to drive more carefully [i.e., make a complete stop at the intersection so that when you hand your money to the politician it doesn't blow away in the wind]. According to Christopher DeMuth, lawyer, scholar, past president of the American Enterprise Institute, and head of deregulation under President Reagan, debate is missing over the use of regulation of the economy. Regulation is a substitute for direct taxation to pay for government policies that would not survive a legislative roll call—efforts, for example, by the Environmental Protection Agency to regulate greenhouse gases through taxation and fines because Congresses decline to pass corresponding legislation. See Christopher DeMuth, "The Bucks Start Here," *Claremont Review of Books*, Vol. XIII, No. 3, Summer 2013, p. 11.

7. A nation that imports more than it exports takes in more goods than it gives up. That's profit! Export nothing, import everything—there's the highest standard of living possible, except that it creates a balance of payments problem, dollars paid for imports are not matched by foreign currency from abroad (from the purchase of a nation's exports) which means the nation's central bank is short. To "balance" that shortage, the U.S., for example, will borrow foreign currency by selling U.S. Treasury bonds (sovereign debt) to foreign investors at a higher than market rate of

interest. That high interest rate (charged to taxpayers) creates inflation, which in turn lowers the nation's exchange rate, which, however, makes U.S. exports cheaper, and as demand for them increases, the balance of payments adjusts. That's how markets work; they counter every false move.

8. When nations borrow to pay for normal consumption—food, health care, retirement—they should choose carefully from whom they borrow, i.e., upon default, which barbarians will they least mind walking in? Default they will, because ten percent interest a year (the rate for junk sovereign bonds) increases the original loan by ten percent a year (unless the interest is being paid). By year ten the loan will have doubled. By year 20 quadrupled.

9. Peter B. Kenen, *The International Economy*, fourth edition, (2000) Cambridge University Press, pp. 484-488.

10. Ibid.

11. Ibid.

12. From 1991 to 2002, Argentina pegged its *peso* to the dollar but that only created an illusion of stability. Argentina did not eliminate its underlying irresponsible fiscal policies. In 2002, consequently, it defaulted on $81 billion in debt (at the time, the largest sovereign debt default in history), after which it experienced a severe economic crisis. This, of course, initiated a return to populist politics. Everything Argentina did was wrong and went wrong: price control on domestic energy, reneging on foreign contracts, export taxation, increased public sector employment, and increased public spending. In 2008, private pension funds were nationalized, later, an airline and a major oil company. The reason Argentina depegged the peso from the dollar was to print money to finance itself—resulting in inflation of 28 percent per year. In January 2014, Argentina devalued its currency another 15 percent. See Ian Vasquez, Cato Institute, in *Forbes*, "Argentina's Luck Is Finally Running Out," 1/31/14.

13. Roger Altman, "Blame Bond Markets, not Politicians, for Austerity," *Financial Times*, 5/8/13.

14. In 2014, the world watched Russia invade Crimea, and through its proxies, eastern Ukraine. Economic sanctions were placed on Russia, although the world always wonders, in relation to such crimes—invasion of a country, unauthorized nuclear buildup—if sanctions are too weak a response.

In the short run, they may be. A nation such as Russia (or Iran), with huge oil and gas deposits, runs an economic surplus and may not need to borrow. But that can't last. Under sanctions, nations' currencies devalue (in the short run, a blessing for Russia in that its sale of oil is in dollars, meaning that Russia will have *more* rubles to pay off its domestic debts), but, too, its credit ratings will drop. Interest rates on its sovereign bonds (its national treasury bonds) will rise, as will inflation. The government, forced to spend more on interest, will, in exchange, raise taxes and spend less on citizens' services. And as sanctions continue, there will be fewer markets for Russia's major export, oil and gas, and Russia will start borrowing to keep its economy going—at first from their own national reserves, but eventually from world markets. With inflation, high interest rates, currency devaluation, and capital flight, Russia will sell its bonds at a discount, and pensioners, in turn, will receive less than they planned. Pretty much like Greece. [See "Rosneft Chief Appeals to Moscow for $42 billion Bailout as West's Sanctions Bite," *Financial Times*, 8/15/14. At the time of this article, Russia's government was considering taking that money from the national welfare fund, the fund which supports the country's legacy pension system.]

As the economy slows, it will fall into recession. With recession comes unemployment. In 2001, when Argentina defaulted on its sovereign bonds, unemployment rose to 25 percent. (See Benedict Manda and Vivianne Rodrigues, "Looming default brings back painful memories for Argentines," *Financial Times*, 7/238/14.)

[Russia, however, is a peculiar case. Vladimir Putin knowingly risks sanctions in exchange for his land grabs. Yes, Russian stocks as a result of sanctions will trade at a huge discount

—with respect to the rest of the world, at price-earnings-ratio of 5.2 compared to an average of 12.5 in emerging markets (see Buttonwood, "Trillion-Dollar Boo-Boo," *The Economist*, 7/26/14, p. 60)—but most Russians won't notice: they do not own stock—individually or collectively, as pension funds or as mutual funds (*Ibid.*).]

Finally, is there a downside to sanctions? You decide! As long-term policy, probably not, unless it incites a nation to war. As short-term policy, perhaps yes, if it causes multinational companies to flee. In South Africa in 1984, there were almost 400 multinationals. After sanctions, by 1989, there were 124. Those remaining were bought for almost nothing by South African capitalists. Owners of stock in those companies made between $8 and $9.5 billion [perhaps $50 billion today] as the crashed value of those stocks eventually came back. According to political economist Thomas W. Hazlett, source for the above facts, long-lasting damage was that as American companies and pension funds pulled out, the University of California, for example ($600 million in 1984, at least $3.0 billion today), America lost influence when it was most needed, when South Africa was still an apartheid nation that viewed international capital as a dangerous promoter of economic, thus racial, integration. Thomas W. Hazlett, "Did Sanctions Matter?", *New York Times* OP ED, 7/22/91.

15. The U.S. is unbelievably fortunate to have complete political gridlock. In no other nation is 50 percent of the population economically aware. No other nation has a population willing to stand up for such an abstraction as economic efficiency. [Imagine how better off the world would have been if political gridlock in Germany and Japan had stopped their actions leading to World War II.]

Half the nation may be economically aware, and one would think, therefore, that those in business would be violently opposed to socialism. They're not. Those successful in business generally are not interested in the actions of government: they know how to circumvent regulation. This is the sense in which Ayn Rand's *Atlas*

Shrugged is a fillip to socialism. In the book, Rand expresses her sense of the immorality of socialism, yet concludes with the main argument in all her writings, that society may win individual battles over such things as social security and tax policy, but since those arguments are not based on philosophy, society is going to lose the war. Why? Because socialism is not philosophy, it's a dream.

The classic argument against socialism, an economy with severe restrictions on private property, is that such an economy cannot know what to produce. Without the free exchange of property (land, goods, services), market prices do not emerge. Without market prices, socialist planners have no way to judge value, thus, no way to know in what to invest. After the fall of Soviet communism in 1989, it should not have been a surprise (although it was) that Soviet planners, when asked how they knew what to produce, and how much and how much to charge, responded, "We guessed. We looked to the West and imitated as best we could." [That alone is enough inefficiency to lead both to lowered economic growth and lowered standard of living. The Soviet Union didn't compete with the West, in that it produced nothing for the market except natural resources; it imitated the West.]

The cumulative effect of 70 years of Soviet communism should have been to reduce the Soviet Union to poverty, but the Soviet Union maintained a certain level of wealth by cheating its citizens: it lowered production costs by ignoring *all* environmental safeguards—Russian factories, chemical factories, mines, dumped their untreated waste into the rivers; and the Chernobyl meltdown created hundreds of square miles of nuclear wasteland for no other reason than planners, to save costs, eliminated a concrete containment system.

And the USSR cheated its citizens of the dynamism of a market economy. With no incentive or opportunity to create and invest, entrepreneurs left (if they could) or went into hiding (to surface after the fall as thieves of the nation's resources—stealing what might have been theirs anyway).

Economists are not responsible for the wealth of nations, but they *are* responsible for the poverty of nations. We can let economists play with socialized economies, but we must never let them touch a market economy. We might let economists guide politics, government, into fostering trade, into eliminating obstacles to trade, even let them pretend to predict the end of business cycles (so that nations do not invest resources at the wrong time), but before giving an economist real economic power, consider the following:

> ...he or she needs to know the aggregate level of current consumption, investment and public spending, as well as what the full employment level of output would be. He or she must also know the precise manner in which the multiplier effect will work to translate an increase in government expenditure into an increase in aggregate demand to achieve that full employment level of output. Each step of the analysis presupposes that the detailed knowledge of economic life is readily available to the macroeconomist and that each policy step advocated will result in the precise effect on economic activity that is intended to achieve economic balance at full employment levels. In short, the model assumes what it has to prove.

—Timothy Sandefur *Conscience of the Constitution* (cited earlier) p. 369.

Karl Marx was an economist. Read Appendix C, his Preface to "A Contribution to the Critique of Political Economy," and you will not want such a socialist to lead your country. You may decide that you want no one to lead your country. Plus, to be an economic actor, there is no need to even understand economics.

In *What Should Economists Do?*, Nobel laureate James Buchanan had this to say:

The market or market organization is not a *means* toward the accomplishment of anything. It is, instead, the institutional embodiment of the voluntary exchange processes that are entered into by individuals in their several capacities. This is all there is to it...

—James M. Buchanan, *What Should Economists Do?*, Liberty Press (1979), p. 31.

According to Buchanan, there is only one principle in economics worth stressing: the principle of spontaneous order of the market, the great intellectual discovery of the eighteenth century (and by Lao Tzu, sixth century B.C.: "Nature does not hurry, yet everything is accomplished."). Spontaneous order explains almost everything in life, and most ideas in this book:

There is no relation between income and wealth;*
there is no relation between income and poverty;
there is no relation between income and government;
there is no relation between income and law.

If a nation wants wealth, does not want poverty, does not want government intervention in the life of its citizens, yet wishes respect for the rule of law, it must not attack income.

*[And there is no relation between savings and wealth. The U.S. has a very low savings rate, one-half that of Switzerland, but is still a wealthy nation. U.S. citizens spend almost all their savings on consumption, but the companies that receive that money deposit their profits in the bank. The bank, in turn, lends it for capital projects. What's important is that nations have an entrepreneurial population. Nations with high savings rates but without an entrepreneurial population are not better off. Compare Switzerland to the U.S.:]

	GDP per capita, PPP (Current international $) [2013]	Gross Savings (% of GDP) [2012]**
China	11,904	51
France	41,421	18
Israel	32,760	21
Japan	36,315	22
Mexico	16,463	22
Saudi Arabia	53,705	47
Switzerland	53,705	33
United States	53,143	17

**www.worldbank.org/grosssavings(%GDP);
www.worldbank.org/GDPpercapita.

16. Jefferson felt pressured to change John Locke's natural right to life, liberty and property, *Second Treatise Concerning Civil Government,* to life, liberty and the pursuit of happiness. Still, it is the Lockean sense that is important, that one has a property right to one's life and to anything one produces: crops, art, goods, services —and by extension, the land used to produce those goods (provided it wasn't stolen). Without private property, which includes enforceable contracts, citizens will not produce more than they need for survival: there will be no surplus, no increase in the standard of living. Witness the current economic success of communist China: it is due to the return of private property to a people who desire nothing more than to produce.

17. Societies based on free individual action are not dependent on the moral restraint of their leaders; they have no leaders—consider the U.S. at its inception (with the U.S. Constitution as a set of rules to restrain government).

If you think leadership is a good idea, look at the great experiment of the twentieth century—the collective organization of society: socialism. To some degree, every nation tried it. Communism, socialism from the Left, and fascism, socialism from the Right (the corporate state), over a short 70-year period were directly responsible for the death of 100 million people. Had the option to switch to capitalism not been there, the death toll would have been higher.

18. What the majority wants is not always legal, constant, or in its best interest. Today the majority live in urban centers, and have, thus, much in common, for example, the fact that living in an urban environment is artificially removed from the natural rhythms of the land. Today agricultural landowners are the minority, two percent of the population; in 1790 they were 90 percent.

The Constitution is structured to give an advantage to the minority. The Electoral College, for example, can (when an election is close) vote for a presidential candidate other than the one who received the popular vote (in that small states have a minimum of three electors no matter what their population); and then, no matter what its population, every state has the same number of representatives in the Senate. Wyoming has a population of 582,000 and California 38 million. Both have two Senators.

> We all declare for liberty; but in using the same *word* we do not all mean the same *thing*. With some the word liberty may mean for each man to do as he pleases with himself, and the product of his labor; while with others the same word may mean for some men to do as they please with other men, and the product of other men's labor. Here are two, not only different, but incompatible things, called by the same name—liberty…The shepherd drives the wolf from the sheep's throat, for which the sheep thanks the shepherd as a liberator, while the wolf denounces him for the same act as the destroyer of liberty…Plainly the sheep and the wolf are not agreed upon a definition of the word liberty.
>
> —Abraham Lincoln, (in Timothy Sandefur, *The Conscience of the Constitution*, Cato Institute (2014), p. 1)

Written in 1864, Lincoln's speech can be seen as a warning to the majority not to trample upon the minority—when the Civil War should end, perhaps for the North not to walk over the South.

Lincoln's speech and the 14th Amendment, both written in 1864, are a reminder that, in this nation, the first duty of government is to protect individual liberty. It is also a reminder that the word *minority*, like *liberty*, needs an agreed-upon definition.

So, too, the word *liberalism*. Liberalism does not mean the Democratic Party in America. That's populism. Nor does it mean what the French think it means—a fanatically free market. Liberalism is a protean set of beliefs in progress, skepticism towards authority, and respect for the individual—the underlying permutation of modern democracy.

19. Legislative gridlock is a fundamental price of freedom. In the U.S. it has occurred regularly. In fact, it led to the Civil War. So, too, is eternal vigilance. Citizens must be on constant alert to recognize threats to democracy—why we have public education—and must be in constant readiness to prevent violence anywhere in the world that has the potential to come here—why we have a strong military.

20. "An American judge armed with the right to declare laws unconstitutional cannot compel the people to make laws, but at least he can constrain them to be faithful to their own laws and remain in harmony with themselves." Alexi de Tocqueville, *Democracy in America*, ed., J. P. Mayer, trans. George Lawrence (New York: Harper Perennial, 1969), p. 269 (as cited by Timothy Sandefur, in *The Conscience of the Constitution*, p. 152).

21. Timothy Sandefur, *The Conscience of the Constitution*, Cato Institute (2014), p. 154.

22. Progressivism is European socialists advocating the use of government, science and technology to organize and improve a nation's social and economic development. The Progressive Caucus is the most liberal wing of the Democratic Party. [John Dewey, B. F. Skinner.]

23. Op *cit*. p. 21.

24. Ibid, p. 25.

25. Years later, Chief Justice Benjamin Cardoso admitted that the Supreme Court reversed its opposition to the New Deal literally because the justices were afraid of Roosevelt. How is that different than the courts in Nazi Germany and the Soviet Union, against their conscience, giving Hitler and Stalin the legislation they wanted?

26. The Libertarian stance is that services such as Social Security, Medicare, Medicaid, and public education—all well-intentioned—should not be administered by the state. They should be administered by the private sector; government should not develop the economy, not provide welfare to the poor (food, clothing, housing, health care), welfare to the middle class (interest on home loans as a tax deduction), and welfare to business (subsidies, tariffs, investment tax credits). Libertarians believe citizens would stand on their own if their tax dollars were refunded. With a low flat tax, business investment would increase, the economy would grow, and citizens, fully employed and well paid, would contribute to charity. The state would provide many types of emergency relief, and temporarily help citizens solve their problems, but not try to solve them permanently. It's not possible to do for someone what they can only do for themselves—eat, sleep, stay healthy, study, show up for work. Open-ended relief— welfare—only leads to prolongation of the problem. The state can provide public education to help the disadvantaged, but the disadvantaged have the responsibility to take advantage of public education by attending class and studying—and if they don't, they shouldn't be allowed to attend. [This is controversial, but consider what Frederick Douglass said: Douglass warned *not* to cater to those who may not make it on their own (referring to newly freed slaves)—not to artificially tie a rotten apple to the tree to prevent it from falling. Speaking to a white nation, Douglass said, "Don't tell us what to do anymore. We are sick of being told what to do. All we ask is that you not prevent us from exercising our rights." Robert M. S. McDonald, "Frederick Douglass: The Self-Made Man," in *Cato's Letter*, Fall 2011, Cato Institute.]

Example: Why is health care in the U.S. so expensive? Because government alone is trying to solve the problem—except that government intervention in the health care market has completely destroyed that market: employers write off employee health insurance premium as a tax deduction, which leads employers to choose the most expensive health insurance possible; it's illegal to purchase health insurance in a state other than where you live which, for example, makes health insurance in New Jersey three times the cost in Pennsylvania; Medicare and Medicaid have increased demand for health insurance well beyond their funding level, which is a large portion of the U.S. budget deficit (projected for 2014 by the Congressional Budget Office to be $642 billion, www.cbo.gov/publication/49172, although, according to Dodd-Frank accounting, Medicare, Medicaid and Social Security are the bulk of the *real* U.S. budget deficit, government's unfunded liabilities, $86.8 trillion for the year ending December 31, 2011, [$123 trillion, 2020] see "Cox and Archer: Why $16 Trillion Only Hints at the True U.S. Debt," *Wall Street Journal Opinion*, online.wsj.com/news/articles/ sb10000142412788732332045781273740390877636); and most importantly, there is no incentive for consumers to bargain health care pricing as they do for *every* other good and service purchased. The result: health insurance is no longer health insurance: it is prepaid health care and costs three times what it would in a free market. In 1965, before Medicare and Medicaid, health insurance cost less than auto insurance. Today, the entire automobile costs less than health insurance.

We have the Affordable Care Act because 40 million Americans were without health insurance. But we also have the act because President Obama is a pragmatist—he chose to work within the system rather than change it. The president argued the commerce clause gave him the power to mandate that everyone buy health insurance, and that the enumerated powers gave him the right to provide the means to pay for it, i.e., increase the budget deficit.

Does the commerce clause really give Congress the right to mandate an activity in order, then, to regulate it—in this case, an inactivity, people refusing to buy health insurance? Or did the President exceed the enumerated powers? Chief Justice Roberts is correct when he said, "The framers gave Congress the power to regulate commerce, but not to compel commerce." According to Elia Shapiro, who provided the above quote, one of the legal team that argued against the Affordable Care Act before the Supreme Court, "The commerce clause is not a general license to regulate the individual from cradle to grave simply because he will predictably engage in particular transactions [not take care of himself]. Even if the individual mandate is necessary to the act's insurance reforms, expansion of federal power is not a proper means for making those reforms effective." (Elia Shapiro, lecture at the Cato Institute, recorded on DVD in 2012 by the Institute for Humane Studies at George Mason University.)

According to Shapiro, for the first time in modern jurisprudence since the New Deal, the court found a federal law unconstitutional—that it exceeded Congress' spending power. The question the court asked, in that the 10th Amendment states that power not given to the government remains in the hands of the people, is whether the financial inducement offered by Congress is so coercive as to pass the point at which pressure turns into compulsion. Government cannot command the people to do its bidding, i.e., buy health insurance whether they want it or not.

With that reasoning, the Court agreed that Congress could not force states to increase spending for Medicaid coverage; Congress had no right to withdraw *all* funding (something Franklin Roosevelt would have done) if a state didn't accept the new regulations, didn't accept the transformation of Medicaid and the further expansion of government.

27. If government can mandate that no one commit a tort, why can't it mandate that citizens act responsibly—purchase health insurance, for example?

Government can mandate that citizens not commit a tort because that is the one law humans need if they are to live together in society—the right to their own life, liberty and property. They do not, however, have a right to food, clothing and shelter. Those are not natural rights; they are natural *needs*. A right to food, clothing and shelter is a right to someone else's property [see income redistribution], and no one has that right.

28. With growth of government, there is loss of individual freedom. There is no way to stop the growth: political careers are founded upon the expansion of government services.

29. The Libertarian stance is that if Congress would mind its own business, there would be no special-interest groups; Congress should stay out of our social lives (as per the American Civil Liberties Union), stay out of our political lives (except to enforce the Constitution), and stay out of our economic lives (literally, enforce the commerce clause, Article 1, Section 8, Clause 3—the enumerated powers clause, which precludes active government intervention in the economy).

30. Voters, too, are disorganized. They have little incentive to make the effort to seek information about what politicians and special-interest groups are doing. They know that their vote is unlikely to determine the outcome of an election and, so, with what in political economy is called "rational ignorance," simply vote their party ticket—hoping their party made an inquiry. [For an intriguing analysis of the inefficiency of voting, see Appendix G, "Arrow's Paradox."]

31. Sandefur, p. 83.

James Buchanan and Gordon Tulloch, in *Calculus of Consent*, warn of the difficulties of defining what is in the public interest, that there are differences among individuals, that value is subjective. Yet, without strict adherence to a constitution, subjective value becomes "progressive" value, in turn, "value-to-be-determined," in turn, "judge-each-case-on-its-merit." Thus, interests rather than law shape society, countering the proposition of John Adams who said we are not a nation of men, we are a nation of laws.

[Progressives treat rule of law as if it were rule of thumb. They do not take the Constitution literally. They see the

Constitution as a living, ever-changing document, and that with respect to American social injustice and inequality, as the cause, not the cure. When it comes to achieving a certain outcome, progressives believe that the ends justify the means, that procedure trumps principle.]

32. James Gwartney, et al, *Microeconomics, Private and Public Choice*, Thomson South-Western (2003), p. 139.

33. Ibid, p. 139.

Electricity generated by Hoover Dam is sold to residents in California, Nevada, and Arizona at rates ten to 25 percent below market. That was legislated in 1937 when Congress agreed to build the dam. The law providing for the subsidized rates was scheduled to expire in 1987, but before it did, Congress extended the subsidies another 30 years. Every senator west of Missouri voted to continue the subsidized rates. All states will pay for it, but in exchange, senators from California, Nevada and Arizona will be expected to vote for every unnecessary subsidy proposed in every other state. That's what it means for government to hand out resources. [You can't solve a problem by throwing money at it, but you can get a Senate majority.]

Ibid, p. 139.

34. Sandefur, *Ibid*, p. 142, endnote 118.

35. Sandefur p.142.

36. Ibid. A political system should be able to stand up to economic analysis. The extent to which monopoly eliminates competition, if that undermines an underlying free economy, is an ethical issue. The same for government. The extent to which a majority eliminates its competition, a minority, if that undermines the underlying democracy, is an ethical issue.

What economic analysis reveals is that there are times for communal action when, at the margin, at a particular moment for a particular activity, it costs less than private action. According to James Buchanan and Gordon Tulloch, marginal analysis is missing from "classical" analysis of policy-making. (James M. Buchanan and Gordon Tullock, *Calculus of Consent* (first published 1962), University of Michigan Press (2011), p. 321.)

37. Funds for public education increased two-and-a-half times between 1970 and 2000, yet there was a five percent inverse drop in test scores. (Gwartney, *Microeconomics*, p. 468.) The implication is that, one, reduction in funding for public schools would increase test scores and, two, that the problems of public education are so deep that money is not the answer. There is no better example than our nation's public schools of how a narrow vision can drive an entity into the ground.

38. Sandefur, p. 87.

39. Ibid, p. 85.

40. Thomas Jefferson, *Jefferson: Writings Letters*, p. 1426, *Ibid*, p. 116, endnote 66.

41. Sandefur, p. 119.

42. Ibid, p. 76.

43. The exact quote: "It has been said that democracy is the worst form of government except all the others that have been tried." Also by Churchill: "The best argument against democracy is a five-minute conversation with the average voter."

44. Ibid, p. 126, endnote 34.

45. "We're all in this together." "It takes a village to raise a child." These progressive expressions are a million miles away from the idea of spontaneous creation, life where survival of the species is a function of independent trial and error, adaptation rather than improvement, pursuit of one's personal interests as a function of economic prosperity and individual liberty: ideas at the heart of Western thought. Coming together other than as a direct democracy (which itself existed only once, in Athens), runs the risk, even as a democratic republic, of creating a society run by elites, an aristocracy, rejection of which is precisely what the United States of America represents.

That rejection began in a meadow called Runnymede in 1215, where it emerged embodied in the Magna Carta, and reached full flower in Philadelphia, in 1787, in the U.S. Constitution—

doctrinal documents which embed two radical premises: one, that our rights come not from kings or queens—or presidents—but are a function of natural law, by which individuals derive certain unalienable rights among which are life, liberty and property; two, power comes not from the top down, but from the bottom up, from "We the People..."

From these unalienable rights we have developed: elected parliaments, *habeas corpus*, free contract, equality before the law, open markets, an unrestricted press, freedom of religion, and jury trials. These things are not somehow the natural condition of an advanced society. They are, according to Daniel Hannan, in *Inventing Freedom* (as cited by Mark Tooley reviewing the book in *American Spectator*, Jan-Feb 2014, p. 64), "specific products of a political ideology developed in the language in which you are reading these words. The fact that those ideas, and that language have become so widespread can make us lose sight of how exceptional they were in origin." Today we not only take them for granted, but consider them culturally specific. The expression, "We're all in this together" is really just left-wing mantra, lame philosophical cover for the idea that ideas from other cultures, for example, the search for communal solutions to societal problems— social security, public education, health care, even economic equality—are equally as relevant. All of that has been tried. It's called socialism, the *raison d'être* of the twentieth century: communism from the left, fascism from the right, multiculturalism from the center. What a waste! What a rejection of the warnings of James Madison, author of the Constitution and of its clauses for checks and balances in government. He wrote, 225 years ago (in *Federalist Paper No. 10*, penultimate paragraph) that the very purpose of checks and balances was to thwart the "rage...for an abolition of debts" (Argentina and Greece today); for the equal division of property (consider William Bradford, Governor of Plymouth Colony 1621 to 1657, writing in *Of Plymouth Plantation* that the society the Pilgrims created, with equal division of land, in which it was forbidden to trade or sell one's share, was a complete disaster and therefore abandoned); and for any other improvement or wicked project…" (American socialism: The New Deal, The Great Society).

46. *Ibid*, pp. 126-127.

47. The Constitution does not provide for public education. "Enumerated powers" allow Congress or the states to collect taxes to pay for services such as public education, but not to provide it. Those who advocate keeping our current system of government-administered public schools do so with progressive rationalization, that a voucher system would relegate the poor to the worst schools (although that is exactly how it is now) because the poor cannot fend for themselves. Again, this is elitist underestimation of the poor, equating poverty with a lack of intelligence, a rise in social services with a rise in intelligence. Why would anyone who sees students walking down the street—well-dressed, books under the arm, not misbehaving (too badly)—not ask, "What school are those children attending? That's where I want my child to go!"

[Middle-class progressives will never admit it, but their "solidarity" with the poor and working class is all in their heads. I was once told by a musician living in Berkeley, California ("a Progressive and proud of it"), who had moved into a racially mixed neighborhood that he was well accepted by his neighbors (believing that they understood he understood their plight) and that for three years in a row had been invited to their Fourth of July barbecue. "After that," he said, "they stopped inviting me. I don't understand why?" I asked, "Did you ever invite them to your house?" Dead silence. It never occurred to him to do so.

That "it never occurred to him to do so" is a conceit. French political economist Frédéric Bastiat put it this way: there is a difference between the gardener and his trees, between the inventor and his machines, between the chemist and his elements, between the farmer and his seeds. The socialist thinks that there is the same difference between him and mankind, as between the potter and the clay [the central planner and the population].* The conceit of the planner, the potter, the elite, the Che Guevaras of this world, is that

215

they rationalize their actions, including murder of the opposition, with the notion that the masses will never understand their vision until it is put into practice. Such an idea, that central planners can organize a nation, is what Nobel Laureate F. A. Hayek calls a "fatal conceit," that the only thing standing in the way of a world free of poverty is insufficient funding and political will.]

*Frédéric Bastiat, *The Law*, The Foundation For Economic Education, Irvington-on-Hudson, New York, 1990 (first published in 1850), p. 35.]

48. Op cit, p. 127, endnote 44.

49. If other nations feel the need to "progress," a need for alternative principles, let them, but not America seek it. Our nation must remain free. It is the only way we will survive, the only way we will attract enough educated and skilled immigrants to replace citizens our public schools are not producing. Immigrants come to the U.S. for one reason (mainly)—economic opportunity, but that opportunity exists only because we uphold social, political and economic freedom, which newcomers experience more profoundly than those who are born here.

50. As defined by Marx, surplus production is capital (the free trade of which is capitalism).

51. Buchanan and Tullock, p. 201.

52. Ibid, p. 209.

53. Political reality is that policy makers prefer to focus on rules for choosing constitutional decisions rather than rules for the allocation of resources. *Ibid*, p. 210.

54. Politically, the U.S. is either way behind or way ahead of the rest of the world. Time will tell. Progressivism or libertarianism, eventually one will prove to have been a reactionary force.

[Consider: all nations have social, political and economic problems yet because their cultures are different, their problems are different. All nations, however, make the same error: they try to solve social and economic problems through the political process.]

Nations do not question such indiscriminate use of politics because they do not think of the governmental process as having its own problems, that government workers just as those in the private sector are guided by self-interest and respond, therefore, to incentives far removed from the problem being solved—legislators, for example, trading votes, agreeing to fund services they would never agree to except that, in exchange, other legislators agree to fund services they want; plus, legislators succumbing to the pressure of those rent-seeking special-interest groups who finance their electoral campaigns. See endnote *33*, Chapter 4, "Basic Laws of Government," for funding of the Hoover Dam.

The choice is not between the real world of markets and the ideal world of government intervention. The choice is between the real-world operation of markets and real-world operation of the political process—why political solutions to social or economic problems do not work, why socialism does not work, why planned economies do not work. That's because the only economic model that does work, the most fundamental economic model—price is a function of supply and demand—even that model cannot possibly incorporate all the information that exists, billions of bits that change billions of times per second. The ability to use such a model is absolutely beyond the reach of any human being (any central planner). At best, individual producers and consumers at a particular moment in time for a particular project, by referencing price, extract the specific information they need. That's how a free economy works: spontaneous individual action.

55. Banks are a Ponzi scheme. They don't have the money they loan; like finance companies, they lend what they borrow. They borrow short term (from the Federal Reserve, from their depositors), loan long-term, then, hope that they will attract new depositors.

When a bank loans money long-term at six percent, it will borrow at five percent, except that if rates rise, it may have to pay seven percent. *That* scenario causes financial instability: leveraging

217

deposits, loaning more money than what is on reserve.* A home buyer who makes a ten percent down payment and borrows the balance is leveraging that down payment and faces the same risk. After years of timely payments, should the homeowner lose his or her source of income—the job—he or she loses the house. That is why banking is regulated, why we have the Federal Reserve: to prevent the hardships that come from financial collapse. [Whether that's possible is another subject.] So, why isn't Congress regulated? Why is Congress allowed to borrow to pay its bills [U.S. budget deficit], allowed to leverage its tax receipts toward investment in the nation's future, yet by doing so, place the nation at risk? Why doesn't legislation such as Dodd-Frank address the public sector?

   * In a socialized economy, government, not banks, causes financial instability. In the name of economic justice, leveraging the poor out of poverty, government orders banks to break sound lending practice and provide loans to those who do not qualify. (President Clinton's ordering of Fannie Mae and Freddie Mac to purchase subprime loans is the perfect example.) Why is *that* not addressed by Dodd-Frank?

   56. Leverage works like this: one firm invests its own $50,000 to earn $5,000, a 10% return. Another firm invests only $10,000 and borrows $40,000 to earn $5,000 less $2,000 (the 5% interest it pays to borrow the $40,000) which equals $3,000, a 30% return. This second firm will then cut its prices so that its return drops to 15%. This price cut will drive the first firm out of business.

   This applies to banks. Banks cannot choose not to leverage; they would be competing with banks that do, banks that cut their prices, lower their rates for lending, or, which is the same thing, raise their rates for savings. Unleveraged banks will lose their customers and be bought up.

   This means that speculation and financial bubbles are not primarily a function of greed, but a function of leverage and overextension of credit. It means that financial bubbles are part of a modern economy. Short of communism, there is no way to prevent them.

57. Capitalist and communist economies have the opposite problems: capitalist economies have labor shortages and recklessly overproduce (then, go into recession); communist economies have labor surpluses and seriously underproduce (yet never go into recession).

The psychological well-being of never having to worry about life's basics—food, clothing, shelter, health care, education, employment—is the attraction of communism. The trade-off is the loss of social, political and economic freedom.

58. National Center for Education Statistics, U.S. Department of Education, nces.ed.gov/fastfacts/display.asp?id=66.

59. See David Parker, *Economic Commentary on the Budget of the San Francisco Unified School District*, master's thesis in economics (2003), Golden Gate University library. (Numbers were adjusted for inflation).

60. No one ever mentions that if the Federal Housing Authority (FHA) in the 1930s had never initiated amortized mortgages for the purchase of a home, allowing a home to be purchased with a five to ten percent down payment, which created not only the ability but also the demand for everyone to own a home, home prices today would not be double what they otherwise would be (in the same way that Medicare and Medicaid increased the demand for health care such that the price of health care has not simply doubled, but tripled). Wouldn't society be better off if $250,000 homes cost $125,000 and were paid for by saving $12,500 a year for ten years? Why pay $450,000 for a $225,000 mortgage for a home worth only $125,000?

61. China's government is Machiavellian. It grants economic freedom in exchange for complete social and political control. Bismarck.

62. Is there a downside to high wages? Yes. Workers with only average skills are unemployable. Unions will try to keep their wages up, but that only forces industry to automate, to replace labor with capital. *That* explains why Europe, despite strong labor unions, is competitive on world markets: Europe invests in capital-intensive industry. *That* has made European labor productive (although unemployed).

63. Come to the dark side! Come; join me and Nelson!

When Nelson Mandela was released from prison in 1990, he told his followers in the African National Congress that he believed in the nationalization of South Africa's main businesses. "The nationalization of the mines, banks and monopoly industries is the policy of the A.N.C., and a change or modification of our views in this regard is inconceivable," he said at the time.

Two years later, however, Mr. Mandela *changed his mind* [this author's italics], embracing capitalism, and charted a new economic course for his country.

The story of Mr. Mandela's evolving economic view is eye-opening: it happened in January 1992 during a trip to Davos, Switzerland, for the annual meeting of the World Economic Forum. Mr. Mandela was persuaded to support an economic framework for South Africa based on capitalism and globalization after a series of conversations with other world leaders.

They changed my views altogether," Mr. Mandela told Anthony Sampson, his friend and the author of *Mandela: The Authorized Biography*. I came home to say: "Chaps, we have to choose. We either keep nationalization and get no investment, or we modify our own attitude and get investment."

"Madiba then had some very interesting meetings with the leaders of the Communist Parties of China and Vietnam," Mr. Mboweni [Governor of South African Reserve Bank] wrote, using Mr. Mandela's clan name. "They told him frankly as follows: "We are currently striving to privatize state enterprises and invite private enterprise into our economies. We are Communist Party governments, and you are a leader of a national liberation movement. Why are you talking about nationalization?"

—Andrew Sorkin, "How Mandela Shifted Views on Freedom of Markets," *New York Times* 12/10/13

64. Why not create one purely red and one purely blue state? Citizens with strong feelings one way or the other (liberal/conservative) could move there. Those states would be a laboratory for exposing the imperfections of each approach, possibly revealing where a basis for compromise lies.

65. If the Constitution is to be interpreted to mean that a highly qualified (i.e., elite) leadership be given power to lead the nation forward, *that* is a return to aristocracy. In this sense, progressivism is reactionary, literally un-American.

Since 1970, thanks to such elite leadership, the U.S. has more than doubled funding for public education although, in inverse relation, test scores have dropped. [See James D. Gwartney, *Microeconomics*, 10th edition, (2003) Thomson Learning, p. 468 and endnote 7, Appendix D.] Since 1950 we've increased spending on social welfare to match that of any socialist nation although poverty has increased from 15 to 22 percent (which we don't see because it is covered over by the social spending). [See Charles Murray, *Losing Ground: American Social Policy 1950-1980*, (1984) Basic Books, p. 65.]

In 2012, the federal government spent $668 billion to fund 126 separate anti-poverty programs, with state and local governments spending another $284 billion, bringing total anti-poverty spending to nearly $1 trillion—which amounts to $20,610 for every poor person in America. Even if that amount is justifiable, how is it that we spend so much and achieve so little? Over the last 50 years we have spent more than $16 trillion to fight poverty—although 15 percent of Americans still live in poverty, no better than the 15 percent living in poverty at the time of President

221

Johnson's first State of the Union address promising an "unconditional war on poverty in America." And today [and continually since 1965] nearly 22 percent of children live in poverty compared to 23 percent in 1964. See Michael Tanner, Cato Institute, *Fox News Channel*, "War on Poverty at 50 – Despite Trillions Spent, Poverty Won," 1/8/14.

66. In California, we force everyone, employed or not, legal or not, to purchase auto insurance if they want to register or drive an automobile. To the Department of Motor Vehicles, affordability is not an issue, not an excuse. Why? Because auto insurance is affordable; government has not intervened in the market for auto insurance.

67. Financial independence is the goal (in 10 years). Otherwise:

> BOSTON — Abe Gorelick has decades of marketing experience, an extensive contact list, an Ivy League undergraduate degree, a Master's in businesses from the University of Chicago, ideas about how to reach consumers young and old, experience working with businesses from startups to huge financial firms and an upbeat, effervescent way about him. What he does not have—and has not had for the last year—is a full-time job [2014].
>
> Five years since the recession ended, it is a story still shared by millions. Mr. Gorlick, 57, lost his position at a large marketing firm last March. As he searched, taking on freelance and consulting work, his family's finances slowly frayed. He is now working three jobs, driving a cab and picking up shifts at Lord & Taylor and Whole Foods.
>
> "I'm not in my basement, unshaven, unshowered, drinking a bottle of Scotch a day," Mr. Gorelick said. "I'm out there working these jobs, meeting people and

trying to make something happen. But it is exhausting. It is stressful. It is difficult."

For people experiencing such long spells without appropriate work, it is a crisis. Often, it is also a conundrum: What should a worker who finds himself out of a job for six months or more do?

"There is this very pressing issue," said Ofer Sharone, a sociologist at the Massachusetts Institute of Technology, "and there is this great gap in knowledge about what to do about it, both for policy makers and these individuals." Should long-term jobless workers seek out career counseling? Should they accept far lower salaries? Should politicians revamp training…

—Annie Lowrey, "Long Out of Work, and Running
Out of Options," *New York Times*, 4/4/14

In other words, in a world of rapidly changing technology and consumer demand, try this for the future:

Age 5 – 25: Learn your first career, work at it for 20 years;
Age 45 – 55: learn your second career, work at it for 20 years;
Age 75 – 95: Start a third career (or a combination of the two), but do not retire.

With the invasion of robots ("rise of the machines"), with the probability that human life will be extended 50 to 100 years, coupled with the possibility of forced leisure at an early age—with a world in which the demented are pacified by stroking robotic seals (which respond with a purr)—retirement is not a good idea. Neither is having to look for a job. Solve that problem within the first ten years of your professional life by achieving financial independence.

68. Rent control is a conspicuous example of a restraint of economic freedom. For example, if the rent of an apartment is controlled at $335 a month when market rent is $1,500, the owner

is deprived of $13,980 ($1,165 x 12) a year, deprived of private property: rent. The tenant is also restrained. A tenant willing to pay higher rent cannot legally negotiate with the landlord (for improved service, for example). Both are socially restrained, as by the San Francisco Board of Supervisors announcement, in January 2004: "Except in a public safety emergency, even light verbal discussion between landlord and tenant is harassment of the tenant." A landlord asking, "How are you, today?" means, "Are you healthy enough to still reside in the apartment? When are you leaving?" All the above is an abuse of political freedom.

69. In the late 1960s, Alice Waters and a few friends wanted to start a restaurant. Alice asked her father for a loan. Her father said, "I won't give you a penny unless you have an option to buy the property." People have always been surprised that one of America's most famous restaurants, Chez Panisse, never charged exorbitant prices. It never needed to. Waters' creative input and the effect that had on the neighborhood caused the value of the underlying real estate to rise [not to mention that the loan paid off].

70. If you believe that labor has intrinsic value (the labor theory of value), that salary should be a function of the time and skill that went into the production of a good or service, you will advocate for a minimum wage. But wage is a function of the supply and demand for labor; it may have no relation to the skill of the worker: an Olympic gymnast earns $10,000 a year, players in the NBA may earn $1,000,000 a year.

There is no evidence that minimum wage helps those who are least well-off. Rather, the effect of minimum wage is to eliminate low salary, entry-level jobs that millions of people are willing to perform. Consider that in the U.S., only 11 percent of workers among the least well-off are affected by an increase in minimum wage. Why? Because two-thirds of those workers live in households that are already two to three times above the poverty line; plus, minimum wage overlooks the fact that the primary problem of the poor is that they are not working enough, not that they're not earning enough. (See David Brooks, "The Inequality

224

Problem," *New York* Times, Op-Ed, 1/17/14, in which he cites Joseph J. Sabia and Richard V. Burkhauser. Their relevant work is "Minimum Wages and Poverty: Will a $9.50 Federal Minimum Wage Really Help the Working Poor?" (2010) *Southern Economic Journal*, 76(3), pp. 592-623; who, on p. 593, cite the *March Current Population Survey* [U.S. Census Bureau] for the 11 percent figure. And they cite *AP-AOL* [Associated Press-America Online polling service] 2006 for the following two quotes:

> Proposals to increase the minimum wage are politically popular because they are widely seen as an effective way to help the working poor. In his statement of support for an increase in the federal minimum wage, President Bill Clinton captured this majority view with, 'It's time to honor and reward people who work hard and play by the rules...No one who works full-time and has children should be poor anymore' (Clinton and Gore 1992)," p. 592.

> [This same thinking was later used to rationalize giving the working poor a home of their own by Clinton's order to Fannie Mae and Freddie Mac to guarantee, i.e., to purchase, subprime mortgages, the direct cause of the 2008 financial crisis.]

Similar reasoning holds that the problem with our nation's public schools is that not enough money is spent on them, that bad public schools in low-income neighborhoods prevent people in those neighborhoods from an equal education. The reality is that public schools in those areas are bad because students in those areas are bad (badly prepared for life), and as a result, good, even idealistic teachers and administrators all eventually leave. Money has nothing to do with it: no matter what the neighborhood, all public schools receive the same per-pupil allowance (within a school district)—not to mention that American public schools receive the highest per-pupil allowance in the world.

Why can't students from low-income neighborhoods get ahead? The problem is not low income or inequality of education, the problem is low social environment. Children from low social-economic backgrounds, from age zero to three (when all learning takes place, when the brain is programmed to receive enormous amounts of information) are not stimulated with *direct* conversation (not words transmitted from a television set or even from adults talking to each other—about Plato), which means they enter kindergarten with a 2,500 to 4,500-word deficit (which educators know, yet never acknowledge, but which does explain why Head Start preschool education has absolutely no effect: it's way too late.]

71. When it appears that a communist country is providing health care and institutions of learning, Cuba, for example, it is because the country either has wealth from natural resources or is being subsidized by a country that does (or is devoting all its resources to those two services). Wealth in a communist country does not come from the production of its citizens; it comes from natural resources. If *all* nations were communist, no nation would produce beyond subsistence, and the world's standard of living would slip back to that of the Middle Ages.

72. "Lunch with The FT: Jagdish Bhagwati,"*Financial Times*, 4/19/14.

73. Peter J. Boettke, *Living Economics: Yesterday, Today and Tomorrow*, The Independent Institute (2012), Chapter 20, "The Limits of Economic Expertise."

74. Cited by John Micklethwait and Adrian Wooldridge in "The Fourth Revolution," *Cato Policy Report*, Vol. xxxvi No. 4., July 2014. Taylor's remark was made one hundred years ago. Yet, 1914, 1776, 5th Century Athens, really, those dates are yesterday.

Appendix C

1. Nobel laureate F. A. Hayek* defines socialism as the belief that deliberate regulation of all social affairs must necessarily be more successful than the apparent haphazard

interplay of independent individuals; that it is easy to improve upon the institutions of a free society, which people believe to be the result of mere accident, the production of historical growth [*cf.* German historicism], which might have occurred completely differently [rather than as the culmination of thousands of years of trial and error, as the best that society can do]; but warns that the means to secure socialism can easily be used for other purposes, equality of income, for example, except that it can also be used to secure inequality, where the means of production are redistributed from private ownership to a new elite, a privileged new class— workers and managers rather than manufacturers. *F. A. Hayek, *Socialism and War: Essays, Documents and Reviews, (The Collected Works of F. A. Hayek) Volume 10*, edited by Bruce Caldwell (1997) University of Chicago Press, pp. 53, 61. Hayek adds, p. 183, that central economic planning presupposes a much more complete agreement on the relative importance of the different ends than actually exists [as if a blanket formula for general welfare actually exists], and that new rulers will not eventually take over the fundamental ideas and methods and turn them to their own needs. [*Animal Farm, Atlas Shrugged.*]

2. Another downside of socialism is that citizens contribute so much to government, the state, that a country's creative entrepreneurs leave. Socialist nations lose, thus, tax and philanthropy from entrepreneurial fortunes, for example, the recent single-person donation of $400 million to Harvard University, or billion-dollar donations to Stanford University used to provide full scholarships and fully paid housing for students in need. Socialist nations also lose private universities, hospitals, libraries, and art patronage.

3. Karl Marx, *Das Kapital*, (1996) Regnery publishing.

4. Perhaps all nations should experience socialism. Otherwise they will always wonder if in *their* case, it might have worked, that *they* could have avoided socialism's greatest problem: shortage. Sweden, a rich nation that did not shut down its private sector (although forcing it to turn over 50 percent of its profits),

could not avoid shortage. Marriage ceremonies entailed formal sign-up to a wait-list of up to 18 years to obtain an apartment (because married couples had preference over single persons). *Caveat*: once a nation goes down the road to socialism, without iron-willed leadership, it cannot come back. See Appendix E, Margaret Thatcher.

5. Capital is surplus production. Free trade of capital is capitalism. Both definitions are by Karl Marx. But their portent is clear: increase capital and you increase standard of living.

[Capitalism and communism have the opposite problems: capitalism recklessly overproduces, has labor shortages and cyclically crashes; communism recklessly underproduces, has labor surpluses yet never crashes. Which do you prefer, a surplus of designer boutiques, or a shortage of uniforms?]

6. There is nothing like personal financial risk to focus your thinking, nothing like financial catastrophe to mold your character, to reveal who you really are.

7. The Laffer Curve reveals that an economy can expand without government budget deficits, that lower taxes lead to lower prices, thus, higher output, thus, higher government revenue.

8. Police, fire departments, courts and public education are paid from property taxes. A nation's military and congress are paid from income taxes, but could be paid from a value-added tax (a tax on consumption) plus a low flat tax.

9. Worldwide, tax havens hold about $20 trillion. See "Tax Havens, the Missing $20 Trillion," *The Economist*, 2/16/13.

Appendix D

1. John Maynard Keynes, *The General Theory of Employment, Interest, and Money* (New York: Harcourt, Brace, and World, 1936), p. 94.

2. Most economists are intellectual. None like (though may secretly admire) the animal nature of an entrepreneur—but that's because their intellectual capacity blurs their judgment. The great economist Armen Alchian begins a major work with the following obtuse opening sentence:

A modification of economic analysis to incorporate incomplete information and uncertainty foresight as axioms is suggested here.

—Armen Alchian, *Economic Forces at Work (A Collection of Selected Works), Liberty Press 1977.*

Couldn't he wait a few pages before scaring his readers away? Why not simply state that the workings of an economy are so full of uncertainty that it's not possible to analyze an economy? Why pretend there are axioms that warn of incomplete information? Why not simply state that uncertainty and incomplete knowledge are a condition of life, part of the dynamic of an economy, precisely what successful participants develop a sense for?

Worse, Alchain compares the success of an economy's dynamic agents to the colliding of electrons, to the randomness of a probability distribution—that business is essentially the result of trial, error, luck, and the ability to adapt to the environment. Archian argues that economic success is not a function of profit maximization and rational behavior [true], but of luck and adaptive behavior—except that he goes on to say that throughout the dynamic process, the economist's rational ability "to predict, explain and diagnose" is not affected. Why? Because economists are not confined to the limitations of the dynamic process. *There it is*: the intellectual elitism of a central planner—fascist or communist, take your pick.

3. In *White House Years, the First Volume of His Classic Memoirs*, (2011) Simon and Schuster, Henry Kissinger states that the President of the United States must be fully prepared before entering office: things happen so fast that it's not possible to learn on the job. Former U.S. Senator Bill Bradley said that the most important preparation for a politician is broad experience: learn and do everything.

4. As Machiavelli advised princes, so too, in China, 2,000 years earlier, did Lao Tzu. Like Machiavelli, Tzu told princes to

stop fighting each other and give the masses some peace and freedom. They will be so grateful that *they* will take care of your needs; *they* will run society for you. The approach (perfectly entrepreneurial): "Nothing is done, yet everything is accomplished."

Wu wei er wu bu wei
無為而無不為

5. Richard Branson, "The Art of Taking Risks," *GEW Magazine*, The Financial Times Ltd., publisher, 11/17/14, p. 3.

Was Branson's vision too simple? Are there any businesses that do not stress the importance of good customer service? In a competitive market, how can firms survive without offering good service? They can't. Firms start off well, become complacent, drop standards, and finally are driven out of business—except the airline industry, where poor service is the norm.

In October 2014 I flew from Denver, Colorado, to Sheridan, Wyoming. Our luggage and rifles were not on the plane when it landed. The personnel at the airport said they would arrive with the next flight, and said to call at 8:00 p.m. to confirm, then, come back and pick them up (from Buffalo, Wyoming, 35 miles away—70 miles round trip) because they offered no delivery service at night. We called at 8:00 p.m. only to get an answering machine. We couldn't instruct them to deliver the luggage to the hotel by 6:00 a.m., where a concierge would accept them. The next morning they did not call to say the luggage had arrived. At 7:00 a.m., after several attempts, we got through. They said, "Come and get'em, but come quickly; the airport closes in an hour." [Yes, the airport was small—but not that small.] The hunt was ruined for that morning.

Branson is correct. Offer good service; no one else does. Where are TWA, American Airlines, Eastern Airlines, Western Airlines, Continental Airlines? Replaced by Virgin Airlines.

6. Real estate, for example, is not housing, office buildings, industrial complexes; it is square feet of property.

7. James D. Gwartney, *Microeconomics: Private and Public Choice*, 10th Edition, (2003) Thomson South-Western, p. 468. The author also notes (p. 468) that in 2000 the United States spent $7,764 per secondary pupil, 38 percent *above* the OECD average, but that eighth-grade mathematics achievement scores in 2001 were 3.3 percent lower than the OECD average (citing OECD, Education at a Glance, 2001).

Average Combined SAT Score, 1967–1999

The achievement scores of American students dropped in the 1970s, changed little in the 1980s, and rose modestly during the 1990s.

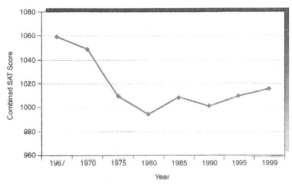

Source: Statistical Abstract of the United States, 2000.

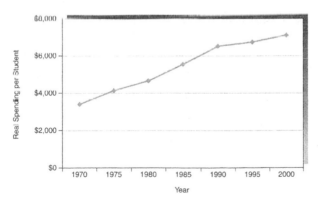

Real Spending per Elementary and Secondary Pupil, 1970–2000

Real spending per pupil on public elementary and secondary schools more than doubled during the 1970–2000 period.

Source: Statistical Abstract of the United States, 1993 and 2000 and www.nea.org.

8. In France, Sarkozy won the 2007 presidential election in part by campaigning in London, where, in order to do business, 100,000 French entrepreneurs [and their families] had moved. [In 2017, estimated at 300,000. See "Brexit Vote Stems Flow of

French Bankers Heading for London," *Financial Times*, 10/18/16.] Unconscionable for a nation to allow that to happen.

Appendix E

1. "Margaret Thatcher - No Ordinary Politician," *The Economist*, 4/14/13, p. 26.

See also the "rotten apple" speech by Frederick Douglass referenced paragraph one of endnote *26,* "the libertarian stance," Chapter 4, "Basic Laws of Government." Both speeches reveal that "progressive" thought in the 1860s was the opposite of "progressive" thought in the 1960s, why progressives today should not quote Abraham Lincoln or Frederick Douglass.

2. Ibid.

3. Cited by Joseph R. Gregory in "Iron Lady Who Set Britain on a New Course," *New York Times*, 4/9/13.

4. Margaret Thatcher would have liked the Jefferson quote:

"A government big enough to give you everything you want, is big enough to take away everything you have."

Appendix F

1. Karl Marx, A Contribution to the Critique of Political Economy, Progress Publishers, Moscow, 1977.

Appendix G

1. Ben Shapiro, *How to Debate Leftists and Destroy Them*, David Horowitz Freedom Center, Sherman Oaks, CA (2014), p. 4. See also CNN Politics, "Exit Polls," www.cnn.com/election/2012/results/race/president.

Appendix H

1. Thomas Piketty, *Capital in the Twenty-First Century*, (2014) Belknap Press of Harvard University.

2. Does income inequality undermine democracy? The classical argument is that inequality reduces trust in political institutions, reduces voter turnout, increases polarization between political parties, and increases the influence of the rich on policy-making. But why wouldn't inequality do the opposite? Why wouldn't inequality increase voter turnout, bring a nation together?

3. Piketty is in league with columnists such as Paul Krugman of the *New York Times*, a Nobel Prize economist, who also writes as if he were not an economist, to a population not educated in economics.

Chris Giles, an economic editor of the *Financial Times*, has verified Piketty's collected data (which is impressive and not way off base) but does not conclude that there is much evidence for the idea that wealth inequality has been rising in the rich world over the last several decades. See Patrick Brennan, "Are There Problems with Piketty's Data? Of Course," *National Review Online*, 5/23/14, www.nationalreview.com.

4. Piketty admits (p. 86) that per capita output and population growth were the same over the period 1700 to 2012: 0.8 percent per year on average. Then he agrees that per capita output was 1.7 percent between 1980 and 2012, with 1.8 percent in Europe and 1.3 percent in America, a little higher than Africa at 0.8 percent (a politically correct statement in that Bolivia and Guatemala are also America, but disingenuous in that no statistic was provided for the U.S. alone). Source of this data is Piketty's private data bank: piketty.pse.ens.fr/capital21c (p. 94). Since Asia logs in at a high of 3.1 percent, we can assume that Piketty's other statistics are low, that Piketty has not proved his point that the rate of growth of capital exceeds that of the economy.

The rate of return on venture capital, capital at risk, may exceed the rate of growth of the economy, but that, too, is meaningless in that worldwide most capital sits in banks unused. Scarcity of viable capital projects explains why the New York Stock Exchange, even real estate in San Francisco and New York, is so overpriced: demand is worldwide. Add the fact that the world's economics are so over-indebted (or corrupt or socialized), all of which creates capital flight to the U.S., and one should not be surprised if the world's economies all come tumbling down.

Appendix I

1. Ayn Rand, *Atlas Shrugged*, (1957) Penguin Group 2005 edition, p. 731.

2. Rand's quote is harsh, but not in relation to what she is referring to, Marxian socialism. Rand also means society has no right to take another person's productive work, achievement that gives value and purpose to his/her life, and give it to someone else. To Rand, giving is not a social obligation. *Ibid*, p. 1062.

> ...Productiveness is your acceptance of morality, your recognition of the fact that you choose to live—that productive work is the process by which man consciously controls his existence, a constant process of acquiring knowledge and shaping matter to fit one's purpose of translating an idea into physical form, of remaking the earth in the image of one's virtues—that all work is creative work if done by a thinking mind... *Ibid*, p. 1020.

Thinking in pure terms, as does Ayn Rand, as did Adam Smith, that society is not organized by design or by government, but spontaneously, when everyone independently pursues their own interests, makes it clear that business and social responsibility are two separate matters. Thomas Jefferson knew that democracy could not survive if society fears giving the vote to every citizen. So, too, Rand knew that charity cannot survive if society fears placing that responsibility directly upon citizens. In other words, the extent to which we fear individual freedom, as in opting for socialism, is the extent to which we lose individual freedom. That is the tradeoff, always.

With her strong beliefs, Rand is incorrect only in reducing life to the concrete Aristotelian notion of A = A, that something is either true or it's not. Irony also exists, the idea that both the truth and its opposite are true, the reconciliation of which is Eastern philosophy.

Plus, there is fate, the idea that you cannot control the thoughts that enter your head, those reminders that tell you who you are. You may ignore them and pursue a career based on anything you desire, but if what you desire are not your normal thoughts, your chosen career may not make you happy. In this sense, morality is choosing to be who you are. As with honesty, so, too, morality is encoded in our genes—for survival. Earn a reputation for dishonesty, and no one will purchase your goods or hire you for your services. You die.

3. The West is not prosperous because it has natural resources [the U.S.A. is the only industrialized nation with large natural resources]. The West is prosperous because its natural resource is its people, those who take the initiative to produce. According to Rand, the world needs to relearn the word, "mine," for that is why we do anything: the personal satisfaction of achievement and possession of the product. This has nothing to do with greed or selfishness, but with individualistic cultures emphasizing achievement over affiliation. The West is prosperous to the extent it refrains from collectivization, from taking from its citizens.

4. Rand, *Atlas Shrugged*, p. 768.

5. Let society compete to prove greater need, with those of greater ability not paid more than anyone else, and citizens will not compete to prove how capable they are; they will compete to convince committees of their sympathetic fellow workers just how needy they are, how entitled they are. Under socialism, where the individual does not have economic opportunity, greed takes the form of working less.

Let societies compete to show greatest ability, where greed takes the form of producing more and earning more, and production will be without limit.

The attraction to the notion of economic justice, as, "From each according to his ability to each according to his need," comes, according to Rand, from jealousy, jealousy of those who earn more than you, more than you think they deserve [which you believe should be shared].

6. Atlas Shrugged is equally a love story written by an excellent Hollywood screenwriter. It ranks number one in the "fiction and literary" category at Amazon and number 15 in overall sales. Total sales in 2009 exceeded 500,000 copies, in 2011, 445,000 copies. The Ayn Rand Institute donates an additional 400,000 copies *per year* to high school students. En.wikipedia.org/wiki/Atlas_Shrugged.

7. Conversation in the teacher lunchroom: "I don't see why we have so many white teachers and staff; we're perfectly capable of running our own schools." ["Why can't they be separate but equal?"]

8. I did gamble correctly in the 1980s. Spineless education bureaucrats in the San Francisco public schools thought they had to fire every teacher in the district if education funding at the state capital was not finalized by a certain date. The funds weren't, and they fired the teachers. Insulted, nervous about their mortgage payments, many never came back.

When the "pink slip" came, I immediately withdrew all the money from my pension and invested it in a four-unit apartment building. That $50,000 investment in $400,000 of real estate, in the early 1980s in San Francisco, is worth today $2 to 3 million, much more than if it had remained in the pension account, i.e., under *public* stewardship. The loophole: if a teacher is fired, even if immediately rehired, he or she does not have to replace withdrawn pension funds.

9. I'm a product of San Francisco public schools and proud of my state. In 2014, I sent $250,000 to the Mississippi Department of Education with the provision that the money be used to raise test scores such that they surpass California. Why? Because that would make California eligible for the world contest for worst-performing public schools, held inappropriately on the island of Guam, where shoeless children sitting on wooden benches, writing on chalkboards, throwing coconuts at each other, scored 50 points higher on the same fourth-grade math test taken by students in California. [Guam, a U.S. Protectorate, is subject to U.S. education

requirements—why citizens of Guam are thankful not to be a protectorate of Japan or China where education requirements are considerably more rigorous.] The check was sent back.

10. Op cit, p. 741.

11. Ibid, p. 783.

12. Ibid, p. 784.

Great art needs great business because they feed on each other; they understand each other. In the U.S., the two great centers of art and business are New York and Los Angeles, the only two cities with a population of 15 million. Business needs that large a population to attract high-level employees (why Silicon Valley, with a surrounding population of only five million, imports labor). And art needs that large a population to attract enough people to purchase rather than simply look at art, or buy posters of same, because artists need to earn a living.

13. Op cit., p. 857.

Appendix J

1. George Orwell, *1984*, (1949) Signet Books, 1977, p. 263.

Made in the USA
Middletown, DE
01 October 2022